TRACK RECORD

TRACK RECORD

THE MOTOR SPORT PHOTOGRAPHY OF
MAURICE ROWE

FOREWORD BY JOHN SURTEES

Q

QUEENSGATE PUBLICATIONS

First published in 1999 by Queensgate Publications

© Queensgate Securities Ltd, 1999

ISBN 1-902655-00-1

To my wife, **Beryl**,
a former secretary at *The Motor*, who brought up our three children
almost single-handedly – as I was so often away – and who spent
so many Sunday nights collecting me from airports and
ferrying me to the office to develop film.

Also, to my great friend, the late **Philip Turner**, with whom
I travelled many thousands of miles. He knew so many drivers
personally, and should have written a book of his own.

CONTENTS

Page 2: Jochen Rindt (Lotus 49B) leads the 1969 Spanish Grand Prix at Montjuich Park, Barcelona.
Pages 4–5: The 1968 International Trophy at Silverstone. Drivers and fans observe one
minute's silence in memory of Jim Clark, killed at Hockenheim the previous week.

John Surtees is still the only man to have won both motor cycle and motor car World Championships, an achievement that is unlikely ever to be equalled. Despite this I always felt that he was underrated as a Formula 1 driver, possibly because he never stepped into a truly competitive car again after he left Ferrari in 1966. It was typical of the Surtees era that a driver with an above average knowledge of engineering would fare best, and John was no exception in this regard. His peers in Formula 1 – Bruce McLaren, Dan Gurney, Jack Brabham and Denny Hulme to name a few – were all first class engineers as well as brilliant racing drivers. Such a combination of skills was almost a prerequisite of the sport.

FOREWORD

READING through Maurice's introduction, I think of so many things that we shared. I, too, recall the V1 flying bombs, and magazines from Temple Press Publications that my father would buy. His collection of *Motor Cycling* and *The Motor*, packed into tea chests, was my favourite reading material during the war years.

The year I won the Formula 1 World Championship – 1964 – also coincided with Maurice's appointment on a full-time basis to *The Motor*, and his towering figure became a familiar sight around the European Grand Prix circuits. But despite winning the Championship – and believing that there were more to come during the rest of the decade – I don't look back upon that period as a decade of excellence. It was a time fraught with indecision on the part of the governing body, starting with 2½-litre engines, changing to 1½-litres and then reverting to 3-litres. Cars started the period technically superior in concept but inferior in engineering quality. Many friends and colleagues were lost as a result, a fact that is brought home so clearly when I leaf through the pages of this book.

But it was not all doom and gloom. There was the arrival of engines from Coventry Climax and, later, Cosworth, which were to form the platform upon which the British Formula 1 industry was built. There were British drivers dominating the world's tracks, and names such as Lotus, Cooper, Brabham, BRM and McLaren dominated the Grand Prix scene on relatively small budgets.

It was a very different world from the modern Formula 1 circus. You often started up your race car in a local garage, and drove it down to the circuit as there were no pit garages. You had two mechanics per car if you were lucky. The public largely went where they wanted and photographers didn't always use long lenses; sometimes they stood on the edge of the track. This informality is captured in Maurice's revealing shots of a period which I suppose could be seen as the birth of the multi-million pound British motor racing industry as we know it today. And if the 1960s witnessed the origins of this industry, then the following decade would herald a complete transformation of the sport into a massive business with a global audience, enormous budgets and safety levels that would never have been dreamt of.

Today, because of the interest in historic racing, you have many so-called experts expounding about the events of the time. People who certainly escaped my notice. But Maurice was there and pictures don't normally lie. I wouldn't agree with all of the comments he makes or some of the views expressed but, as I have said, he was there and this is part of his life's work. It is a valuable contribution to the recording of times gone by.

JOHN SURTEES
Edenbridge, Kent

Hurry up and take the picture Maurice! Surtees – the reigning World Champion by the time this picture was taken – prepares to steer his Ferrari out of the Silverstone pits while yours truly *(centre)* dithers over shutter speeds.

It's quite unusual to see me in the winner's circle at all: print deadlines at *The Motor* generally meant that I had to be away from the circuit with my films long before the race had finished. The *Daily Express* banner in the background points to the fact that this was a 'home' event, where time was on my side.

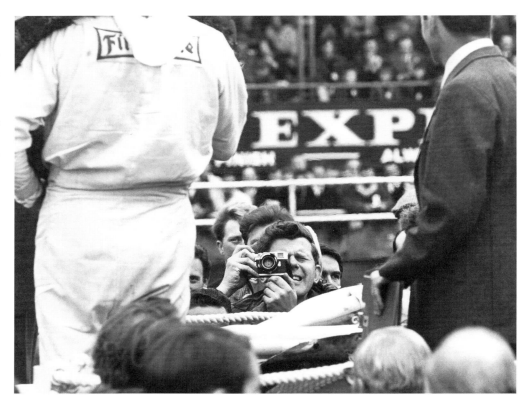

The Press Stand at Le Mans in 1953, my first trip to the great race.

INTRODUCTION

WHAT I really wanted to do was join the RAF.

I spent every waking moment dreaming about it. I joined the Air Training Corps and visited many RAF and USAF airfields to try and scrounge a seat on whatever winged wonder happened to be going out that day. I even managed to hitch a five-hour ride in a Lancaster bomber flying out of Waterbeach, a truly exhilarating experience that simply confirmed my passion for aviation. Anyone of my generation will tell you how difficult it was to find a job in London during the last months of the war, particularly if – like me – you were just 17 years old. It was my love of flying that got me started.

I suppose you would have called me 'an anorak'. I studied *The Aeroplane Spotter* and collected aircraft recognition books. I used to read *The Aeroplane* magazine avidly; you might even say religiously. Anything to do with planes, I lapped it up. And one day I took it upon myself to turn up on the doorstep of the publisher of *The Aeroplane* – Temple Press, Bowling Green Lane, London EC1 – just to see if they would give me a job. It was simple as that.

The man in charge of the Temple Press foyer, Sgt Berry, was rather taken aback by my request. He looked me up and down a couple of times and eventually said, 'You could try the photographic department. I think they need an office boy.'

'But I'm not interested in photography,' I explained. That wasn't good enough for Sgt Berry who, with a ruthless efficiency that would ultimately become very familiar to me, was on the telephone to the relevant department.

The head of photography was an elderly gentleman by the name of Tom Rowe. When I told him my name was also Rowe he insisted that I accept the job, despite the fact that I continued to say that I wasn't interested. He said that I would make an excellent photographer because I was very tall and would therefore be able to take pictures over the top of a crowd of people, which I suppose had a certain logic to it. Funny to think that I would later be instantly recognisable to fellow journalists as 'the bloke with the stepladder.' Anyway, I took the job. It was 1944.

My main chores in those early days were drying prints on a rotary glazer, copying silhouettes of aircraft on a massive copying camera and – inevitably – making the tea. The war was still very much in evidence and I used to cycle to the city from my home in Earl's Court with V1 flying bombs clattering overhead, making a noise like a ramshackle motorcycle. The Germans had also started launching V2 rockets from Holland and from the top floor of the office we could trace their vapour trails as they shot into space. But the bomb that remains firmly embedded in my memory was the one that hit Smithfield Market, only a few hundred yards down the road. The tremor seemed to lift Temple Press several feet off the ground.

This picture of the French driver, Benoist, was taken by my boss – and namesake – Tom Rowe, who offered me a job in the Photographic Department of Temple Press. The race was the 1935 French Grand Prix at Montlhéry. Benoist – pictured here hanging on to the bonnet of his Bugatti 59 – was a hero of the French Resistance. He was murdered, strangled by piano wire, in 1944.

My trusty VN Press Camera which I used throughout the 1950s, and the early part of the 1960s. With only two dozen 9cm x 12cm plates available with which to photograph an entire race, there is no doubt that the VN concentrated the mind. Exposure was determined by setting the width of the focal plane shutter and winding up the clockwork tension. There was a scale riveted on top of the camera from which – by cross-reference to width of blind plus tension – you read off the shutter speed. I suppose you could say it was a bit like shooting with a muzzle-loading rifle.

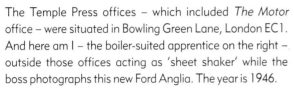

The Temple Press offices – which included *The Motor* office – were situated in Bowling Green Lane, London EC1. And here am I – the boiler-suited apprentice on the right – outside those offices acting as 'sheet shaker' while the boss photographs this new Ford Anglia. The year is 1946.

I was drafted into the National Service in 1947, joining the Fleet Air Arm as an air mechanic working on Supermarine Seafires 17s and Fairey Fireflies based first at St Merryn, Cornwall and later at Ford, in Sussex. When I returned to Temple Press two years later my mentor and namesake, Tom Rowe, had retired and Charles Sims, one of the leading air-to-air photographers, had taken over. All vacancies had been filled by ex-Service personnel during my absence, but my old job was secure thanks to a government ruling that all firms were to rehire staff once they had done their National Service.

I had motorised transport, too, in the form of a Triumph Tiger 100 motorbike. The purchase was a smart move on my part. The independence my new wheels afforded me meant that I was soon dispatched to all kinds of events armed with one of the company cameras – a VN Press Camera or a Leica. It was at this point that I first started to take photographs for the weekly car magazine, *The Motor*, one of around a dozen titles owned by Temple Press.

The 1950s came and went and I became ever more established on the unlikely career path of press photographer. I was working for all the Temple Press publications, including *Motorcycling*, *Cycling*, *The Motor* and *The Aeroplane*. The diversity of jobs on offer meant that I could be sent anywhere from a cycling velodrome to an aircraft carrier. I made regular trips to Le Mans from 1953 onwards and covered the World Cycling Championships in Reims and Paris; I was sent out in a Fairey Gannet to photograph the *Ark Royal* at sea and even scooped the first-ever pictures from the cockpit of the Russian Tu-104 jet airliner. For a confirmed aviation enthusiast and burgeoning petrolhead, life in the photographic department of Temple Press was very heaven.

The turning point came in 1964, when *The Aeroplane* and several other titles were closed down and the threat of redundancy reared its ugly head. I was fortunate enough to be offered the first choice of two plum photography jobs – one on *The Motor* and one on the surviving aviation title, *Flight*. Despite my love of aircraft the decision was not that difficult. Motoring was clearly a growth industry and I had made many good friends on the magazine.

Strangely enough when I joined *The Motor* on a full-time basis it was very much with a wait-and-see attitude. I had no idea that the job would last me another 25 years.

The photographs in this book cover what I think many will agree was a unique period in motor sport. From Alberto Ascari at the height of his powers through to Frank Williams just starting out with his fledgling team – via Stirling, Jimmy, Bruce, Jochen, Niki, Ronnie and the rest of them – I think I have most of it covered. Hopefully it isn't too much of a cliché to say that we'll never see anything like it ever again. Which is just as well, I suppose. We all – regular fans as well as those directly involved with the sport – lost far too many friends.

MAURICE ROWE
Barnet, London

Thirty-five years later the job remains the same but the camera equipment has changed somewhat. This is Le Mans in 1988 and my faithful stepladder continues to provide excellent service.

The start of the 1958 International Trophy at Silverstone. Peter Collins' front-engined Ferrari gets the jump on the rear-engined Coopers while Stirling Moss *(hand in the air)* has stalled. Collins won, but those Coopers wouldn't be kept at bay for much longer.

FORMULA 1

The first motor race I ever covered for Temple Press was at Goodwood in June 1952. Le Mans winner and former Colditz resident Major A P (Tony) Rolt is nearest the camera, at the wheel of Rob Walker's Delage, next to the man who would become Britain's first-ever Formula 1 World Champion, Mike Hawthorn.

The 1953 British Grand Prix at Silverstone was my first race with a 'proper' international entry and I was an extremely nervous young photographer with a brief to get two dozen plates of this important race back to the *The Motor* office in London by the following morning. All eyes were on the young Hawthorn (pictured here leading Felice Bonetto's Maserati) in this race. He had just returned from an historic victory over Juan-Manuel Fangio in the French Grand Prix at Reims, and now the knowledgeable crowd was hoping for a 'home' win. Unfortunately Hawthorn lost control at *Woodcote*, his Ferrari 500 being pitched into a lurid spin that scattered the photographers gathered there. He was able to recover, but after a subsequent pit stop rejoined in last place. He climbed back to fifth at the end but the victory went to his Italian team-mate, Alberto Ascari.

Competition from the home teams during the 1953 British Grand Prix came from men such as garage owner Ken Wharton in the Cooper-Bristol, although I must admit the chances of him actually *leading* Fangio's Maserati – as this picture seems to claim – are extremely small. He finished the race ten laps down.

Back to Goodwood for the traditional Easter Monday meeting; the year is 1954. This is the start of the last race of the day, the Glover Trophy. Nearest the camera is the young Scot, Ron Flockhart, in his first season as an official BRM driver. Wharton is next, also in one of the Bourne cars, and Tony Rolt is 'on' – as *The Motor* press reports used to say – the Connaught (no 45). The rear wheel disappearing from the frame belongs to Reg Parnell's Ferrari, which led for the opening laps but failed to finish when the gear lever came off in Parnell's hand with the gearbox stuck in neutral.

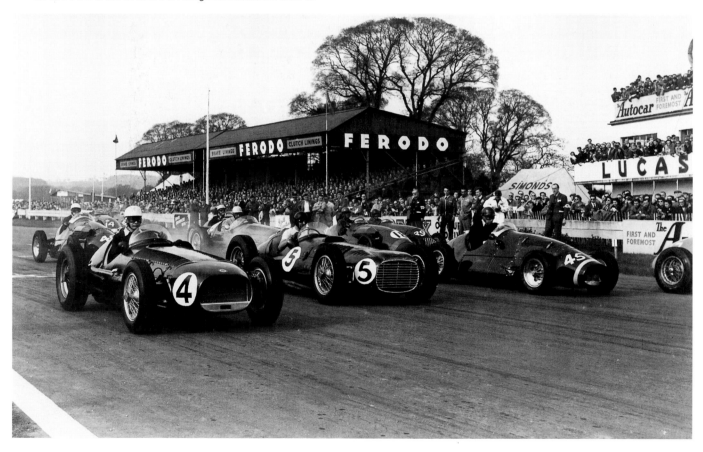

Formula 1 first came to the North of England in May 1954, when the Grand National steeplechase course at Aintree hosted the inaugural non-Championship Aintree 200. The circuit played host to the British Grand Prix the following year – won by Stirling Moss – and went on to alternate with Silverstone until Brands Hatch took over in 1964. The photograph shows the field diving into *Tatts Corner* at the start of the first Aintree 200. Peter Collins' 'Thin Wall Special' Ferrari leads from Flockhart in the BRM (left), Reg Parnell's Ferrari, Roy Salvadori's Maserati (behind Flockhart), Jean Behra, Ken Wharton and the rest. Moss, with his new Maserati 250F, won the race after Collins retired from the lead.

Alberto Ascari returned to Silverstone in 1954 to defend his British Grand Prix title. He was on leave from Lancia to drive this Maserati 250F, but he had arrived with his friend and team-mate, Luigi Villoresi, too late to start official practice and so the pair were forced to start the race from the back of the grid.

This is Villoresi in the sister car. Both he and Ascari were storming through the field in fine style when Ascari – the reigning World Champion – had to pit with engine trouble and fell back to last place. It was at this point that I had my first taste of the teamwork that existed in Formula 1 in those days. Learning of Ascari's problems Villoresi duly pitted and handed his car over to his team leader.

And here is Ascari – now in Villoresi's car – valiantly fighting to get back on terms with the opposition. But Villoresi's selflessness was to no avail: the engine on this car also gave up before the end of the race.

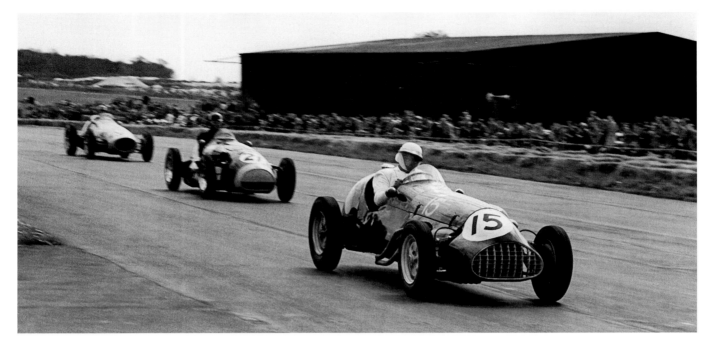

I must confess that Silverstone was a rotten place for photographs. A disused aerodrome, the Northamptonshire track was flat and featureless and there were few points on the circuit where you could take an interesting picture since most corners looked the same.

'All arms and elbows', to steal a well-used phrase. The winner of the British Grand Prix in 1954 was none other Froilan Gonzalez, or 'the Pampus Bull' as he was affectionately known. This giant from the Argentine started his Ferrari 625 from the front row of the grid and led throughout in a race that lasted nearly three hours, trouncing the much-fancied Mercedes streamliners. Gonzalez was always hugely popular in Britain, perhaps because he won his only two Grand Prix at Silverstone.

The principal opposition to Gonzalez came from his old friend and compatriot Juan-Manuel Fangio in the streamlined Mercedes-Benz W196. Of course this was the first time that I – or anyone else in England for that matter – had seen these extraordinary cars. They were not suited to the exposed, blustery circuit and even the maestro himself had trouble keeping it on the black stuff. The dent at the front is the result of yet another brush with one of the many metal marker tubs (filled with earth) that lined the circuit. In fact he left the road on no fewer than four occasions during the race, eventually finishing in fourth place.

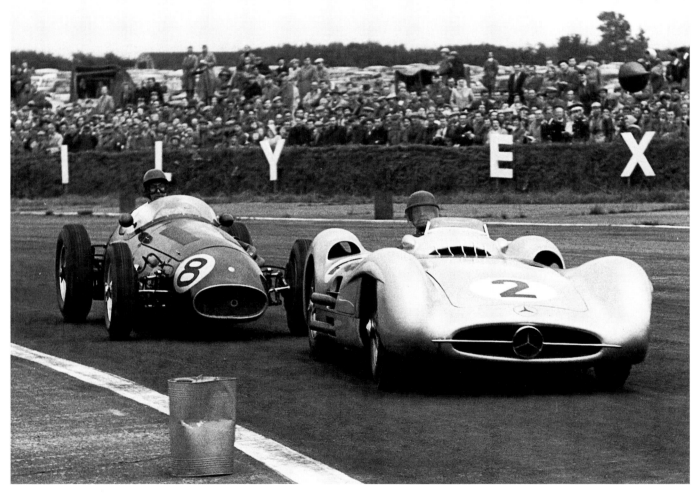

Fangio's team-mate Karl Kling fared even less well, tooling around in the back half of the field while trying to get on terms with his unwieldy mount. Seen here leading Wharton's Maserati 250F, he eventually finished three laps behind Gonzalez. Note the dented metal bin on the inside of the white line.

The Daily Express International Trophy meeting at Silverstone in 1955. The young Prince Birabongse Bhanudej Bhanubandh of Siam – or 'Bira' – passes the burning wreckage of Ken Wharton's Vanwall that had spun at *Copse*, crashed and burst into flames, setting fire to the grass in the process. Wharton suffered burns to the face and neck but survived the ordeal.

The race itself was a thriller, with Roy Salvadori – pictured here at *Abbey* – engaging in a ferocious battle for the lead with Peter Collins. Both men were Maserati-mounted and exchanged lap records throughout the race; Collins eventually took the victory.

You certainly had to trust a driver's skill in those days. Inches away from my feet and travelling far faster than I would like are Harry Schell and Stirling Moss in a pair of Vanwalls. And don't be fooled into thinking that the wall gave me any protection! The venue was Silverstone once again and the event the 1956 Daily Express Trophy. This was Moss' first outing in Tony Vandervell's patriot missile, and the experience would lead to his decision to drive for the team full-time the following year.

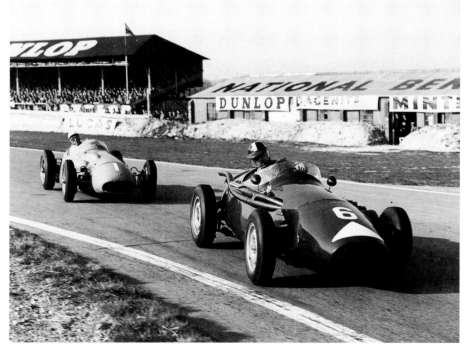

Stirling smiles for the camera before the start of the 1956 Glover Trophy at Goodwood. Extended to 32 laps (about 76 miles), it was the longest race yet to be run at the beautiful Sussex circuit. Moss, Archie Scott-Brown and Mike Hawthorn had a fantastic scrap for the first half of the race. Scott-Brown gamely held off Moss and Hawthorn in the early stages, with Hawthorn 'grinning broadly throughout' according to *The Motor* report. Moss eased his Maserati 250F past Scott-Brown and went on to win the race. Scott-Brown retired with a blown engine on lap 17, while Hawthorn went off in a major way at *St Mary's*. Fortunately he was not seriously hurt.

More smiles at the end of the race as Moss gives Scott-Brown a lift back to the pits.

The 1958 British Grand Prix produced an afternoon of sweet revenge for Enzo Ferrari when his two young English drivers, Peter Collins and Mike Hawthorn, turned the tables on the British Vanwall team to finish first and second in their own backyard. It was Collins – pictured here – who took the victory although his good friend Hawthorn would ultimately win the World Championship. Collins himself was killed in the German Grand Prix barely two weeks after this picture was taken.

Moss – carrying his preferred lucky number '7' – started the British Grand Prix from pole position in the Vanwall but was unable to stay on terms with Collins and Hawthorn. Here he laps Swedish driver Jo Bonnier's 250F as the pair race through *Becketts*. The only consolation for Moss that weekend was winning the sports car race in a Lister-Jaguar.

I always thought it rather foolish to stand with your back to the track while fiddling with your camera, although this chap on the right doesn't seem too worried. Hawthorn's Ferrari is just exiting the shot and following hot on his heels are the Cooper T45-Climaxes of Roy Salvadori and Jack Brabham, and Graham Hill (taking part in his first British Grand Prix) in a Lotus 16.

The third Ferrari at Silverstone that year was run by the young German Count, Wolfgang 'Taffy' von Trips. He drove for the Maranello concern on several occasions between 1956 and 1958, but it was not until 1960 that he joined the team full-time. He was another one whose life was cut short well before its prime. He was killed during the 1961 Italian Grand Prix in a horrific accident that also claimed the lives of 14 spectators.

To get as close as this I was obviously feeling brave that weekend! This is Moss, executing another perfectly-balanced four-wheel-drift.

This fake *montage* (two pictures taken at the same spot joined through the 'A' of the Armstrong banner) was put together in *The Motor* office in an attempt to examine the different driving styles between the two Championship protagonists of 1958, Moss and Hawthorn. Looking at it today I am not so sure that it doesn't tell you more about the handling characteristics of the Vanwall versus the Ferrari... Either way, you are looking at two great talents of the age.

Opposite: Mike Hawthorn and Peter Collins developed a special friendship during their time as team-mates at Ferrari. They nicknamed one another 'Mon Ami Mate' after a character in a contemporary newspaper cartoon strip and got up to all kinds of off-track nonsense. This picture *(top)* shows them at the peak of their achievements together. Mike, on the left, had beaten Stirling Moss to win the French Grand Prix at Reims just two weeks before and now they are both celebrating their '1–2' on home soil. It seems hard to believe that just two weeks later Collins would be dead – killed at the Nürburgring – and his devastated friend would be left 'going through the motions' for the rest of the season. Hawthorn *(below)* picked up enough points to seize the World Championship from Stirling Moss and then promptly retired from the sport. If there was any justice in the world then the story should have ended there, with Hawthorn marrying his girlfriend and enjoying a long life as Britain's first-ever World Champion. But things are never that simple. Hawthorn, who was suffering from a life-threatening kidney disease, was killed in January the following year when he lost control of his powerful Jaguar 3.4 saloon in heavy rain on the Guildford by-pass.

SPORTS CARS

Previous pages and above: I first covered the Le Mans 24 Hours in 1953. My strongest memory from that weekend is of the enormous crowd. Having only covered a handful of races at Goodwood and Silverstone I had never seen anything like it. I positioned myself at the top of the Press Stand for the 4pm start and took these two pictures before heading across to *Tertre Rouge*. It seems incredible today – with 36 exposures on a single 35mm film – but I only had 24 slides with which to cover the first half of the race! I had to be very selective with my shots. At about midnight I would make my way to Le Mans railway station where my colleague Dick Benstead-Smith (who would later become *The Motor*'s Editor) would take the films by train to Paris and then on to London by plane. I can clearly recall more than one occasion in the back of a car at Le Mans station with a blanket over my head, changing slides and taping up the boxes to keep the light out. It was like something out of a spy novel.

I would have taken this night shot just before leaving for the station. I didn't have a light meter or anything like that, the whole process was down to experience – of which I had very little – and guesswork.

A typical Le Mans dawn, with the main straight and the pits complex shrouded in mist. This was taken after I returned from the station with another two dozen slides. It's amazing how many people are still milling around. I seem to remember that the track was still lined with people in most places around the circuit – something of a contrast with later years when you would have to step over sleeping bodies wherever you walked.

The race itself was dominated by the Jaguar C-types that finished first, second, fourth and ninth. This is the Stirling Moss/Peter Walker car – Moss at the wheel – which led for the first hour before an early pit stop put them out of contention. They fought back valiantly to finish second behind team-mates Duncan Hamilton and Tony Rolt.

After the start I made my way across to the *Esses*, which was often a good place for capturing the unexpected. These two shots *(above, and opposite top)* are taken from opposite ends of the complex. The spinning Talbot in the first shot has just clipped the bales and pirouetted in the middle of the bend; the tyre marks seem to tell a tale of driver error and terminal oversteer.

Further through the bend – pointing the *right* way this time – come the Bonetto-Valenzano Lancia D20, the Marzotti brothers' pretty Ferrari 340MM (which finished fifth overall) and an Aston Martin DB3S driven by Reg Parnell and Peter Collins. The Porsche 356 behind them was in the capable hands of Belgian racing driver-journalist, Paul Frère.

The victorious C-type of Hamilton and Rolt. The pace these two characters set during their battle with Ascari's Ferrari was simply breathtaking. Perhaps even more astounding was the fact that they were both nursing dreadful hangovers. Informed by Jaguar boss 'Lofty' England the night before the race that a practice infringement (they were running the wrong number) meant they would not be able to start, the two Englishmen had disappeared to the nearest bar to drown their sorrows – which they did with typical determination. They were found by 'Lofty' in the early hours of Saturday morning and informed that one entry had dropped out and they *would* be able to start after all. Lots of black coffee was ordered – or was it 'hair of the dog'?

Now this is something you would never see today. Rodney Walkerley, Sports Editor of *The Motor*, was allowed to take the Hamilton-Rolt car out for a quick spin the morning after the race. Just look at that caravan in the background…

I visited what you might say was the British version of Le Mans later that year. The 7.4-mile road circuit at Dundrod, near Belfast, hosted the RAC Tourist Trophy for five years between 1950 and 1955, with the event growing in stature every year until it assumed full World Sports Car Championship status. Cresting *Deer's Leap* during Aston Martin's victorious 1953 campaign is Tony Whitehead in the DB3S, which finished fifth overall. This is where, in 1955, Jim Mayers' 'Bobtail' Cooper hit a gate post and burst into flames while he and a group of lower-capacity sports cars were trying to get past a Mercedes 300SL coupe. Mayers and Connaught driver Bill Smith were killed in the ensuing chaos that involved half-a-dozen cars. The TT was never run at Dundrod again.

Spectating at Dundrod was pretty simple: you just wandered across a field and leant against the nearest five-bar gate. Stirling Moss – pictured here in 1953 at the wheel of a Jaguar C-type – was the uncrowned king of this demanding circuit, winning three times in five years.

Stirling's big problem during the 1953 race was tyre wear, as witnessed here by the man himself and – in the white cap – Team Manager 'Lofty' England. The abrasive Dundrod surface meant that treads were thrown all over the course and the leading teams would have to change rear tyres every 20 laps or so. Jaguar had the World Sports Car Championship in mind and ordered Moss to drive for fourth place – and valuable points – rather than chase the lead Aston Martins of Peter Collins/Pat Griffith and Reg Parnell/Eric Thompson.

This point of the Dundrod circuit is no longer used as a public road, as I discovered during a visit in 1992, but it gives you a good impression of the terrain we had to cover in order to get to different points of the course. I spent most of my time clambering over earth banks, stone walls and crawling under barbed wire. Added to those minor inconveniences was the weather, which was almost always lousy. This is 1954 and that little 745cc DB-Panhard is about to be swallowed up by Musso's Maserati and the Moss/Walker Jaguar.

I was back in 1955 for the fateful 50th anniversary race, where the main attraction was the expected battle between Moss in the Mercedes-Benz 300SLR and Hawthorn in the Jaguar D-type. This shot of the start was taken from the pedestrian bridge that crossed the main straight at the bottom of *Rushyhill*. Ninian Sanderson (D-type) leads Hawthorn away from the start while Moss, Whitehead, Castelotti, Trintignant, Fangio *et al* scrabble for position. Moss was in the lead by the end of the first lap and went on to lead home a Mercedes 1–2–3.

Hawthorn took the battle to Mercedes in fine style, snatching the lead after Moss' rear tyre threw its tread and sent the SLR sliding into an earth bank – forcing an unscheduled pit stop. Hawthorn and co-driver Desmond Titterington kept the pressure on throughout the seven-hour race, only losing their edge when the rain started to fall and the advantage swung back in Mercedes' favour. The Jaguar eventually retired from second place with just two laps left to run – a blown engine the cause.

And here is Moss, the rear quarter of his 300SLR bearing the scars of that earlier incident. The Mercedes mechanics had successfully chewed through the bodywork to the satisfaction of the race stewards and Moss – who did the large bulk of the driving despite being paired with John Fitch – set off in pursuit of the leaders. He regained control of the race on the 56th lap and thereafter kept a firm grip on proceedings until the finish.

It seems amazing to see those people standing behind that metal gate, which would surely have flattened them had anything hit it. Back then it didn't seem anything more sinister than a good spot to watch a motor race. Here John Fisher (Kieft) is about to be lapped by Luigi Musso (Maserati).

Leathemstown Corner, leading down to the start and finish straight: the Whitehead brothers' Cooper-Jaguar leads Jean Behra in a Maserati.

Back at Silverstone for the 1955 Daily Express International Trophy Meeting. Desmond Titterington gets away first in the Ecurie Ecosse D-type, followed closely by Tony Rolt. Slow away, but destined to make the running after only a few laps, is Mike Hawthorn (no 1), but the race was ultimately won by Reg Parnell in the Aston Martin DB3S. Car no 37 is none other than Stirling Moss proving his brilliance at running starts by getting away sixth despite starting almost at the back of the grid in the tiny Beart-Rodger.

The sight of someone of Stirling's calibre struggling at the back of the field in an uncompetitive car was highly unusual in 1955 and it speaks volumes about the man that he still gave it his all in the race.

The legendary Archie Scott-Brown, a born fighter who was undoubtedly one of the best drivers of his generation. His deformed arm meant that he was refused an international licence and could not race abroad, but his exploits in a succession of sports cars – most notably the Lister – made him a favourite with press and public alike. I took this picture during the British Empire Trophy weekend at Oulton Park in 1958. Scott-Brown had enjoyed a titanic battle with Stirling Moss (driving an Aston Martin DBR2) in the third heat and both drivers went into the final with their tails up. Moss won outright while Scott-Brown was forced to retire his Lister-Jaguar with a broken drop-arm. Unbowed by this he took over team-mate Bruce Halford's car, stuffed the seat with cushions so that he could reach the pedals, and went on to finish third!

Another larger-than-life character was big Duncan Hamilton, pictured here at Goodwood in a D-type. Hamilton enjoyed his greatest racing successes with sports cars. That popular 1953 Le Mans win was followed by a second place overall the following year and victory in the Reims 12 Hours in 1956.

One of the classic car and driver combinations towards the end of the decade was that of Moss and the Aston Martin DBR1. This highly fruitful partnership produced further victories for Stirling in the Tourist Trophy – now held at Goodwood – in 1958 and 1959 as well as superb back-to-back wins in the demanding Nürburgring 1000kms. Here he is during the 1958 Goodwood TT driving the car he shared with his former Vanwall team-mate Tony Brooks.

The likeable Tony Brooks was one of the few drivers who could hold a candle to Moss and, when they shared a competitive car, they were well-nigh unbeatable – as spectators at the British Grand Prix in 1957 and here, at Goodwood in 1958, will attest.

Aston Martin completed a clean sweep of the podium in this race, helped no doubt by the fact that Ferrari – having already sewn up the Sports Car World Championship – chose not to send a team to the Sussex track. Following in the wheel tracks of Moss and Brooks was the DBR1 of Jack Brabham, pictured here, and Roy Salvadori.

The third DBR1 was shared between the Texan Carroll Shelby and the popular English driver Stuart Lewis-Evans. Lewis-Evans it was who drove the third Vanwall alongside Moss and Brooks, playing a vital role in the British team's Constructors' Cup victory. He was tragically killed in the final Grand Prix of the season – in Morocco – barely six weeks after this photograph was taken.

Many people reckoned that Goodwood was the wrong place to stage the Tourist Trophy – and certainly it was a far cry from places such as Ards and Dundrod. But on a sunny September day it was a wonderful place to be and the popularity of the Trophy itself rose accordingly, as the packed grandstands at the chicane show.

Same race, same place; one year later. It's now 1959 and the World Sports Car Championship is down to a straight fight between Ferrari and Aston Martin. With maximum points on offer in the Tourist Trophy the leading protagonists were forced to send their strongest teams: four factory-entered Testa Rossas from Ferrari and three works plus one privately-entered (Graham Whitehead) DBR1. The wild card of the event was the works Porsche entry, with Jo Bonnier and Wolfgang von Trips bringing their 1600cc Spyder (no 22) home in second place behind the Moss/Salvadori/ Shelby/Fairman DBR1, and just two seconds ahead of the leading Ferrari. Had the Ferrari finished second then the World Sports Car Championship would have been tied between Newport Pagnell and Maranello.

Phil Hill heads a train of machinery through the chicane, including the Maglioli/Barth Porsche (no 23) and the Blond/Sieff Lister-Jaguar (no 8). His 2-litre Ferrari retired early in the race.

Testa Rossa convoy through the chicance during the same race, the Belgian Olivier Gendebien leading American Dan Gurney.

Parting shot from the 1950s: Mike Hawthorn, Britain's first-ever Formula 1 World Champion, and 'Lofty' England, who led Jaguar through its halcyon Le Mans days.

GALLERY 1962–67

Monza, 1963: John Surtees, Ferrari 156.

Le Mans, 1962. The winning Ferrari 330LM of Phil Hill and Olivier Gendebien.

Le Mans, 1962. Class-winning Porsche 1600, driven by Edgar Barth and Hans Herrmann, and abandoned Tojeiro-Climax.

Spa-Francorchamps, 1964. Jim Clark (Lotus 25), at *La Source*, on route to his third successive Belgian Grand Prix victory.

Spa-Francorchamps, 1964. John Surtees demonstrates an eye for detail in his World Championship-winning year.

Brands Hatch, 1964: Ferrari team-mates John Surtees (in foreground) and Lorenzo Bandini.

Graham Hill, five times winner in Monte Carlo, and BRM P261.

Monaco, 1965: Jack Brabham, Brabham BT11-Climax.

Monaco, 1965: John Surtees, Ferrari 158

British Grand Prix at Silverstone, 1965: Jackie Stewart's 'home' Grand Prix debut, driving a BRM P261.

Jim Clark and the Lotus 33 were victorious again at Silverstone in 1965.

Silverstone, 1965: Graham Hill (BRM P261) prepares to do battle with Clark.

Jo Bonnier, Rob Walker-entered Brabham BT7, at Silverstone, 1965.

Daily Express International Trophy, 1965: Mike Spence, Lotus-Climax.

Daily Express International Trophy, 1965: Jochen Rindt, Cooper-Maserati.

Monaco, 1966: Jochen Rindt and Cooper-Maserati.

Monaco, 1966: reigning World Champion, Jim Clark (Lotus 33-Climax).

Monaco, 1966: Richie Ginther, Cooper-Maserati, leads Bruce McLaren, McLaren M2B-Ford.

The road to Reims. Mike Parkes' Ferrari debut was the 1966 French Grand Prix. He finished second.

Reims, 1966: Jack Brabham, Brabham BT19-Repco, *en route* to his third World Championship.

Formula 1 Ferraris at Le Mans – for the French Grand Prix – in 1967.

A little further up the same grid, World Champion Jack Brabham – in Brabham BT24-Repco (3) – waits for the start alongside team-mate Denny Hulme.

Graham Hill at Le Mans in 1967, still to finish a Grand Prix in the new Cosworth-engined Lotus 49.

Le Mans, 1967: Jim Clark, on right, retires. Dan Gurney's Eagle-Weslake races on.

The 1960s was a decade when the realities of this most dangerous of sports registered in all our minds. Jackie Stewart's determination to ring the changes in safety won him few friends, but he was a brave man — as this shot of him at the Nürburgring in the BRM P261 illustrates.

One man who did more than his fair share to cultivate the image of the Grand Prix driver as a devil-may-care extrovert was Innes Ireland, pictured here at the Nürburgring in 1960. The charismatic Scot drove for Colin Chapman from 1959-1961 and his one and only Grand Prix victory – at Watkins Glen in 1961 – was also the first World Championship win for Team Lotus.

Summer of 1961. Front row, from left, Jim Clark, John Cooper, Innes Ireland, Stirling Moss, Graham Hill, Jo Bonnier, Dick Jeffrey, Bruce McLaren and Dan Gurney.

The usually taciturn Jack Brabham was nicknamed 'chatty' Jack by the press; he obviously saved his more expressive side for the race track. He was also known as 'Black Jack' on account of his ever-present five o'clock shadow. This is him behind the wheel of a Lotus 24-Climax during the International Trophy Race at Silverstone in 1962, the year his own Brabham Formula 1 car made its Grand Prix debut.

Poetry in motion. I make no apologies for the number of Jim Clark pictures in this book. The man was a genius after all, and unfailingly courteous. Here he is at the wheel of the Lotus 25-Climax on his way to victory in the 1962 British Grand Prix at Aintree, the first of five wins in his 'home' event.

Monaco, 1963. John Surtees' V6-engined Ferrari 156 leads Bruce McLaren's Cooper T66-Climax down towards the harbour chicane, both men seemingly secure in the knowledge that there are at least a dozen bags of sand to protect them. Note the change in surface on the exit of the corner: these are the paving slabs of the quayside and they were absolutely lethal when wet. This was one of my first trips to Monaco and I'll never forget the moment when I discovered that the cars were clocking 130mph through the speed trap at the approach to this chicane. Surtees finished fourth that year, behind Graham Hill, Richie Ginther and McLaren.

The unmistakable profile of that most British of racing drivers, Graham Hill – looking not unlike a Battle of Britain fighter pilot with his rather tatty helmet and goggles, well-trimmed moustache and rock-solid jaw. Graham was not the most naturally gifted driver by any means, but he possessed an extraordinary drive and determination that saw him collect two World Championships as well as a magnificent five wins at Monaco – a record beaten only by Ayrton Senna.

A chance to relax by the pool during the Monaco Grand Prix weekend of 1965 (above left). I was there for purely professional reasons, obviously. Stirling Moss, now retired from professional driving following his accident at Goodwood in 1962, is on the left next to Kiwi journalist Eoin Young (in sunglasses). Jackie Stewart applies the sun lotion to wife Helen. We would occasionally get the odd celebrity turning up at Grand Prix but nothing like as many as you see today. Of all the races in the Formula 1 calendar Monaco was the one to visit: this is Peter Sellers and Britt Ekland in 1965 (right).

I have always been struck by how relaxed Jimmy Clark looks in this picture, almost as if he is nodding off. Moss was similar in this respect, and both drivers would finish a race as fresh as if it had only just begun.

The battle of the clans: Jackie Stewart versus Jim Clark. People often forget how for the best part of a decade Grand Prix racing was dominated by these two Scots. For ten years between 1963 and 1973 the World Championship went to Scotland on no less than five occasions. In 1968, Clark overtook Juan-Manuel Fangio's record of 24 Grand Prix victories, while Stewart increased the record to 27 wins in 1973. It would be another 14 years before the record was broken.

Nice cardigan Jimmy! Clark leads the parade of drivers down the pit straight to the *The Motor* bridge at the start of the 1965 British Grand Prix at Silverstone. Les Leston was on hand to interview the drivers, although I seem to recall that most of the questioning was directed towards Clark and Stewart and focused in particular on the role porridge was playing in the success of Scots drivers. That's Clark's team-mate, Mike Spence, following.

This is the Italian Grand Prix of 1965, where Clark started from pole and recorded fastest lap, but would ultimately retire. The extraordinary thing about this race was that Clark *didn't* win it. He had won every Grand Prix he had started that year (missing Monaco in order to start the Indy 500 – which he also won). Needless to say, he won his second World Championship that year with consummate ease.

The shadows lengthen at Monza in 1965 and reigning World Champion John Surtees leads this high-speed train in the troublesome flat-12 Ferrari 1512. Following closely in its wheel tracks is Jackie Stewart's BRM P261, Clark's Lotus 33, Graham Hill in the other BRM and Surtees' team-mate, Lorenzo Bandini. Stewart won the race to record the first of what would be 27 Grand Prix wins in an extraordinary career.

The relationship between Lotus founder Colin Chapman and Clark was as close as any you will see in sport, and Chapman was devastated when Jimmy was killed. I remember one year, after the Italian Grand Prix, Colin and Jimmy had heard that a friend of theirs (the name escapes me) was entertaining a young lady in his hotel bedroom. The pair of them found a ladder from somewhere and climbed up on to the balcony outside the room so that they could bang on the shutters and put the man off his stride, as it were. Jimmy then sneaked back down and took the ladder away leaving Colin stuck on the balcony shouting 'Come on Jimmy, this has gone far enough…'

This shot of Surtees' loyal lieutenant, Lorenzo Bandini, at Monza was taken from a makeshift platform erected over the top of the *Curva Parabolica*. It was an excellent vantage point spoilt only in later years as more people discovered it.

Sicilian lawyer and sports car ace Nino Vaccarella, on the right, in discussion with Ferrari Chief Engineer Mauro Forghieri and John Surtees before the start of the 1965 Italian Grand Prix. Vaccarella was an occasional driver for Ferrari, joining the team three times for his 'home' race. Surtees started from the front row but retired with clutch trouble. Three days later he would be fighting for his life in a Canadian hospital following a testing accident at Mosport in a Lola T70.

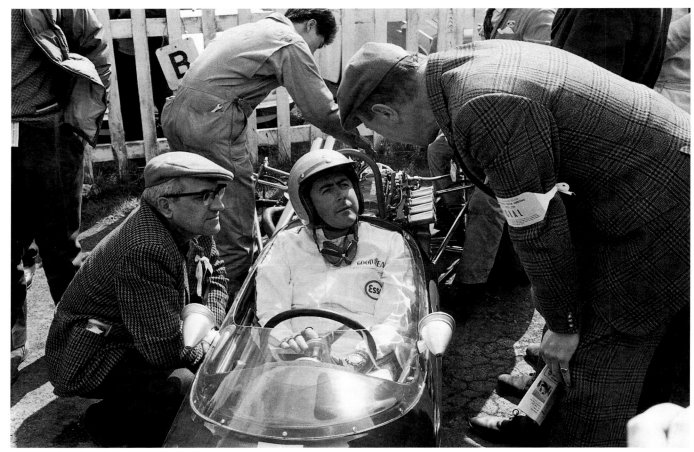

Goodwood Easter Monday meeting, 1966. Jack Brabham receives an earful from one of the race stewards for creeping at the start of the saloon car race. Now he is getting ready to start the single-seater event. It was not unusual for the drivers to race three or four times in one day. Sadly this was the last Easter meeting to be held at the beautiful Sussex circuit. Brabham was running the new Honda Formula 2 engine in his own car; he and Denny Hulme romped home first and second in the Sunday Mirror International Trophy.

Bandini scuffs up his shoes before the 1966 Monaco Grand Prix.
Several of the drivers did that in order to improve their grip on the pedals.

Seconds to go before the start of the 1966 French Grand Prix at Reims. The character in the striped beret is Toto Roche, President of the Automobile Club of Reims. Toto was disliked intensely by both drivers and the press. As the race starter he would take immense pleasure in keeping the drivers guessing as to when the start would be. He would wander up and down the main straight with the starting flag hidden behind his back, gazing casually at the sky. Then without any warning he would bring the flag down and run for his life. It was the ambition of more than one driver to get him but he always managed to reach the safety of the trackside. When the Reims track was finally closed Toto mysteriously disappeared and so – allegedly – did the circuit accounts.

Swiss star Jo 'Seppi' Siffert gives British driver Bob Anderson a lift back to the pits on his Cooper-Maserati during practice for the same race. Anderson was another one for whom we would all soon be mourning; he was killed in a testing accident at Silverstone the following year.

More displays of *camaraderie* during the same French Grand Prix weekend. Jack Brabham gets a helping hand back to the pits from team-mate Denny Hulme. Jack had run out of petrol, but it wasn't a disaster since this was only practice for the Formula 2 race. In fact he went on to win the race itself with ease.

The reigning World Champions, Jim Clark and Lotus, struggled with the new 3-litre regulations in 1966, taking just the one win at Watkins Glen. But the new Cosworth-DFV was imminent and they would be back at the front of the grid before too long.

Clark has to push the Climax-engined Lotus 33 out of trouble after spinning on only the second lap of the 1967 Monaco Grand Prix. Having negotiated the straw bales – and the eager marshal – he rejoined at the tail of the field and went on to make the fastest lap of the race. That wasn't the end of his troubles, though: he later crashed out at *Tabac*. Somehow Jimmy and Monaco just never got it together.

Praying for reliability? The revolutionary Cosworth V8-engined Lotus 49 made its sensational debut at the 1967 Dutch Grand Prix. Graham Hill put it on pole – knocking something like six seconds off the lap record – while teammate Clark, pictured here before the race, won outright.

American legend Dan Gurney on his way to the fourth and last of his Grand Prix victories, this one at Spa in 1967. This race was something of a nail-biter. Jackie Stewart led for BRM, but he had lost fifth gear and was forced to drive with one hand holding the gears in place. Gurney – at the wheel of his own Eagle-Weslake V12 – broke the lap record twice in three laps in order to catch the ailing Scot, taking the lead with just seven laps to go. Gurney was a fantastic driver whose record doesn't do justice to his talent. Arguably the most gifted Formula 1 driver ever to come from the USA, he always seemed to suffer from appalling luck and reliability problems.

The most famous corner in motor sport? *Eau Rouge* was the usual spot from which I would photograph the start of the Belgian Grand Prix at Spa-Francorchamps, then I would work my way back to *La Source* hairpin before leaving the circuit after just one hour of racing. Magazine deadlines meant that I had to catch the Sunday evening plane from Brussels so I never actually saw the end of the race.

They say fortune favours the brave: Clark was man enough to admit that the Spa-Francorchamps circuit frightened him but he still managed to win there four times in succession, 1962-1965. He started this 1967 race from pole in the Lotus 49, but finished sixth after a lengthy pit stop.

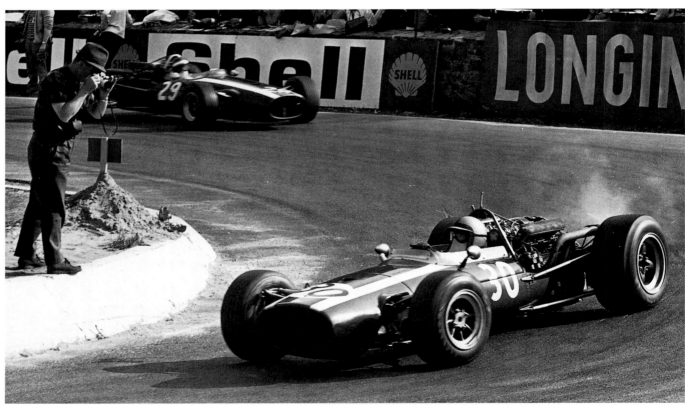

This shot of young guns Pedro Rodriguez and Jochen Rindt – Cooper-Maserati team-mates – at *La Source* hairpin is another excellent example of how close you could get to the track – and to the cars. It amazed me that no one ever fell into the path of an oncoming car. You were also allowed to cross the track in those days: you had to wait for the signal from a marshal that it was safe to cross and then run like mad.

Jimmy's last Formula 1 win at home was at Silverstone in 1967. There were so many photographers there that day that I had had trouble getting a good view, so I climbed up onto the winner's trailer (they used to pull the race winners round behind tractors in those days) and shouted to him. He looked round and gave me this wonderful broad smile which I'll never forget.

I think it would be fair to say that Graham Hill knew the value of a good photo opportunity. I took this series of shots just before the start of the International Trophy at Silverstone in April 1967. You will notice that all the other competitors have driven their cars to the holding area while Graham gets his seven-year-old son Damon to steer the Lotus for him. These pictures hold a special poignancy now, given that both men became Formula 1 World Champions. But the sequence wasn't entirely down to luck: Graham was writing a column for *The Motor* and I had been detailed to get plenty of 'informal' pictures of him, so whenever he saw me coming he invariably did something newsworthy. The funny thing about Hill Snr is that people only ever seem to remember his wit and his charm – qualities he enjoyed in abundance – while the reality was that he also had a very hard side to his nature and people crossed him at their peril.

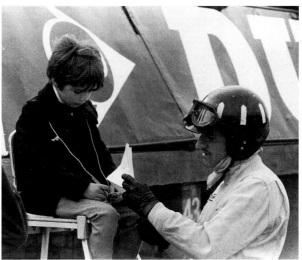

Drivers using all available Nürburgring tarmac, including the pits, at the start of the 1967 German Grand Prix – with Jim Clark (Lotus 49) and Denny Hulme (Brabham BT24) getting away first. It was always a real fight to get to the front of the crowd for a good start picture but on this occasion I must have found something to stand on. Either that or I had suddenly grown several feet.

Another good spot for a close-up at the 'ring was the banked *Karussel*. This shot of Rindt gets you right into the cockpit. He looks pretty relaxed at the moment, I must say, but it didn't last. A couple of laps later the new 3-valve engine in his Cooper-Maserati overheated and dowsed his nether regions in boiling water. The car kept going, however, and the unfortunate Austrian was forced to continue until he retired with steering trouble. Lucky for him, I reckon.

Jackie Oliver's Lotus 48 (running in the Formula 2 category) gets airborne at the Nürburgring. This place was, for fairly obvious reasons, one of my favourite spots to take photographs. It was certainly one of the most exciting. Known simply as 'the 13km post', the cars flew into the air here and if you crouched low enough in the adjoining ditch you could get some quite good pictures. It was too far to walk during the race itself because we would never have got to the airport on time but it was usually worth a visit during practice.

Drivers would occasionally get it wrong at the 13km post and would then have to sit and wait in the middle of the surrounding Eifel forest until practice, or the race, was over and someone could go and get them. This happened to Jochen Rindt one year. His Cooper-Maserati came flying over the hump with all four wheels in the air, landing with such force that the underside was terminally damaged. This picture shows Rindt after the crash, peering out from behind the bushes while practice continues and he waits for a lift home. Once I had finished taking my pictures I took him back to the pits in my hired VW Beetle. Walking back to the car from the track we were surrounded by dozens of German fans all wanting the Austrian's autograph. He jumped into the car, covered his head with a newspaper and shouted 'Race! Race!' to me.

BRM Chief Mechanic Cyril Atkins signals to the eventual winner, Denny Hulme, that he has just one lap to go before winning the 1967 German Grand Prix. Atkins and another BRM mechanic had trekked out to Jackie Stewart's retired P115 to see if they could get it started. Clearly they couldn't, but it provided a useful vantage spot from which Atkins could watch the race unfold.

A good view – from the outside of the *Karussel* this time – of the unusual wooden-chassis Protos-Cosworth Formula 2 cars designed by Frank Costin and driven by Brian Hart and Kurt Ahrens. The wrap-around windshield didn't catch on.

Three successive years of Formula 1 World Champions taken from the same point during the same race: the 1967 Italian Grand Prix at Monza. Jim Clark, the 1965 champion, started from pole in his Lotus 49 but finished third after puncturing early in the race. Jack Brabham, the reigning champion, blasts beneath me in the Brabham BT24-Repco; he finished second. And finally Denny Hulme, Brabham's team-mate, who looks like he is giving a lesson in controlled oversteer while waving at the camera. Denny retired from this race but ended the year as the World Champion – New Zealand's first.

A non-championship race at the new Spanish circuit of Jarama towards the end of 1967 offered little in the way of entertainment until Jackie Stewart managed to get it all wrong right in front of me. He came up to me in the hotel dining room that evening and said 'That was a good picture I gave you today, wasn't it?' I had to agree.

Jochen Rindt looks worried as his mechanics attempt to do something about the failing clutch on his Cooper-Maserati. The event is the 1967 Race of Champions at Brands Hatch, traditionally run in two heats. Rindt switched to team-mate Guy Ligier's car for the second heat, but fared little better.

Rindt, pictured here on the right with Alan Rees (who would later help found the March team), was a pretty cool customer. I remember one year at Monza he agreed to have his heartbeat monitored during practice for a doctor who was doing research into driver's reactions. Rigged up to this contraption Rindt happened to have a colossal spin on the main straight while travelling at something like 130mph. When the doctor checked the readings from the monitor afterwards he discovered that the ice-cool Austrian's heart had scarcely skipped a beat during the incident. This caused endless amusement in the pits.

The 1968 season saw Formula 1 go through a torrid time as it tried to come to terms with the loss of no less than four drivers in as many months: Jim Clark, Mike Spence, Ludovico Scarfiotti and Jo Schlesser. Clark's death on 7 April caused perhaps the greatest shock waves because he was so highly rated as a driver. One minute's silence was held at the start of that year's International Trophy – held shortly after the accident – where the drivers stood by their cars and bowed their heads. The atmosphere when I took this picture was just incredible. There was not a murmur in the crowd, just the solitary note of the lone piper pictured on the right. I was at Brands Hatch on the day Jimmy died in Germany and I can still clearly recall the way in which the news spread through the grandstands, row upon row falling silent. It was extraordinary.

But of course the racing goes on. This is the start of the International Trophy a few moments later, with Bruce McLaren getting away first in the McLaren M7A-Cosworth and the rest of the field enveloped in clouds of tyre smoke.

International Trophy again. Kiwi racer Chris Amon attempts to drive his Ferrari 312 at 150mph without goggles. The fastening strap had snapped, prompting Amon to hurl them at his pit as he drove by. He then spent the next five laps trying to put on his spare pair while racing at the same time. Only Chris could have such bad luck.

John Surtees – having thrown in his lot with Honda by now – leads a serpentine trail of cars around the new Spanish circuit of Jarama. The 1968 Spanish Grand Prix was the first round of the World Championship to be held since Clark's death. Moreover, we were still reeling from the news that Mike Spence – the man who took Clark's place at Indianapolis – had been killed during practice for the American race just days before. The one chink of light in the seeming impenetrable gloom came when Jimmy's teammate Graham Hill, pictured third here behind Surtees and Bruce McLaren, won the race for Lotus.

This is a favourite of mine. Bruce McLaren gives a wry smile to the camera while team-mate Denny Hulme, on the left, discusses tyre choices with the Goodyear technicians and the McLaren mechanics prior to the 1968 Belgian Grand Prix. I like the relaxed nature of the group and the fact that nobody even thought of objecting to my taking a picture. Bruce was running his own team by then and Denny had joined him for 1968 as World Champion. Whatever they eventually decided here, it was obviously the right choice because Bruce won the race!

Following the death of Scarfiotti at the Rossfeld hillclimb only the month before, the Grand Prix fraternity was forced to deal with yet more tragedy when Frenchman Jo Schlesser lost his life during the French Grand Prix at Rouen. Schlesser was an inexperienced driver who had accepted an invitation to race the new air-cooled Honda RA302. John Surtees, Honda's regular driver, had refused to drive the new car because he considered it unsafe, but Schlesser – with everything to prove – agreed to race it. On only the second lap he left the track at one of its fastest points and slammed into an earth bank. The car caught fire and the 41-year-old died instantly. The picture here shows Dickie Attwood and Denny Hulme passing the burning wreckage while the marshals struggle to put out the flames. You won't find many pictures of accidents in this book for the simple reason that I would avoid them if I could. I hated them. I suppose it might have been more newsworthy to file a shot of a burning racing car, but I just didn't want to know. Too many lives were lost and there was rarely anything you could do to help.

Schlesser confers with the Honda engineers before the start of the race.

The conditions during the French race itself went from bad to worse, with visibility reduced to a few yards. This is Chris Amon (Ferrari 312) waving Denny Hulme's McLaren past, but it was wet weather ace Jacky Ickx, Amon's team-mate, who took the race win – principally because he was the only driver canny enough to start the race on 'wets'.

Bruce McLaren takes the McLaren M7A to a magnificent victory in the 1968 Race of Champions at Brands Hatch, proving that the hard-working New Zealander was still capable of performances of the highest calibre despite the pressure of running cars in both Formula 1 and the burgeoning Can-Am series.

Those ridiculous high wings. Still, they often made for an interesting picture, particularly when contrasted with the snakes and squiggles of a beautiful track like Montjuich Park, just outside Barcelona. This is Jochen Rindt leading the way in the Lotus 49B during the opening stages of the 1969 Spanish Grand Prix. Both Rindt and team-mate Graham Hill – the reigning World Champion – suffered massive shunts that weekend at a time when the connection between high wings and high speed accidents still hadn't been made.

Jo Siffert, pictured here on his way to third place at Monaco in the Rob Walker-entered Lotus 49B, was one of the most popular drivers on the Grand Prix scene; his fatal crash at Brands Hatch towards the end of 1971 hit everyone very hard indeed. Another one to start his racing career on two wheels rather than four, the 'Crazy Swiss' formed a close friendship with Walker and scored the first of his two Grand Prix wins at the wheel of Rob's 49B at the 1968 British Grand Prix.

The downhill charge from the *Casino Square* into the right hander at *Mirabeau* on the first lap of the Monaco Grand Prix always used to send my heart racing. Jackie Stewart leads in his Matra MS80 from Chris Amon's Ferrari 312, Stewart's team-mate Beltoise and the Lotus 49Bs of Graham Hill and Jo Siffert. Stewart drove like a demon in this race but it was Hill who ran out the winner for a record fifth time.

Frenchman Jean-Pierre Beltoise can claim the somewhat dubious honour of being the last man to win a Grand Prix for BRM, a feat achieved in monsoon-like conditions at Monaco in 1972, driving the P160B. Here he is three years earlier at Zandvoort in 1969. I don't think that the leather gloves would have protected him against very much, but at least he is belted in.

Bruce Mclaren, also pictured before the start of the Zandvoort race. His death the following year – testing one of his own cars at Goodwood – was a tremendous blow to the sport.

It was always very easy to take portraits of drivers before a race started; certainly you would never get told to push off by anyone. This is Siffert looking very focused. I rather regret not talking to him more than I did. I remember having an awkward conversation with him when he retired his car just near where I was taking pictures, but the moment of a retirement is never the best time to get chatting to a Grand Prix driver!

Chris Amon's helmet looks as if it has seen better days. Funny how, these days, most drivers would probably take two or even three helmets to each race. Amon probably used that for several years!

Jack Oliver's big break in Formula 1 came as Graham Hill's number two at Lotus in 1968. He had a difficult time – crashing two races in succession and incurring the wrath of Colin Chapman – and was quickly replaced by Jochen Rindt. It was all rather unfair since at least one of his accidents was caused by 'high-wing failure'.

Jackie Stewart lifts a wheel through *Abbey* on his way to victory in the Matra MS10-Cosworth. This was the British Grand Prix in 1969 and Jackie's third win in succession. Pictures with a bit of blur about them were absolutely forbidden in *The Motor* office, but as cameras got better and the quality improved we were slowly allowed to experiment with the odd 'speed' shot. They would rarely, if ever, get put in the magazine because the publishers believed that the readers wouldn't like them.

The mercurial talent of Jacky Ickx – pictured here coming in to land at the Nürburgring in 1969 – should have seen him win at least one World Championship. He came close on several occasions but never quite made it. He was the undisputed wet-weather ace of his generation, however. He was also a true gentleman, probably the driver I admired the most of all.

No matter how many times I saw a Le Mans start, I never ceased to be surprised by the explosion of noise. Seconds after the silence and the pitter-patter of feet sprinting across the hot tarmac there would be this most incredible eruption as all the cars fired into life.

SPORTS CARS

This seeming impromptu picnic is, in fact, a drivers' meeting prior to the start of the 1961 Le Mans. Standing on the left is Jim Clark. Other leading protagonists include Phil Hill (sitting on the right wearing a dark T-shirt) and Stirling Moss. The man in the sports jacket with his back to the camera is Peter Garnier, the Sports Editor of *The Autocar*.

Two bright British stars, Stirling Moss and Graham Hill, share a joke during practice for the 1961 Le Mans, where they shared a Ferrari 250GT (only the roof is visibile). They were at very different stages of their careers, however. Moss was an established personality while Hill had yet to win in Formula 1. Incredibly, he would be World Champion within 18 months.

Quickest out of the blocks by a long shot in 1961 was Jim Clark in the Border Reivers Aston Martin DBR1. The Aston following (no 4) is Roy Salvadori in the car entered by John Ogier and co-driven by Tony Maggs, while alongside is the pretty Franc/Kerguen DB4GT Zagato (no 1). The winning *Testa Rossa* (no 10) of Olivier Gendebien and Phil Hill is just behind.

Despite Clark's superb start 1961 was another Ferrari benefit, with the Belgian-American partnership of Gendebien and Hill sharing the winning car for the second time (they won in 1958) and Mike Parkes and Willy Mairesse following them home. This is the Parkes/Mairesse car – Parkes at the wheel – storming through *Whitehouse*. The tail bears the scars of an earlier tussle with the youthful brothers Rodriguez (whose combined age, by the by, was just 39 – less than the individual age of some of the men they were racing!)

Whitehouse again, but this is the Hill/Gendebien car on its way to victory. Look at those people on the right: the circuit would have gone right past their front door.

The finishing ceremony at Le Mans was always rather frantic. During my last few years covering the race I used to get fed up with trying to elbow my way to the winners' rostrum and settled instead in the grandstand with a long lens. At the end of the 1961 race, however, I was right in the thick of the action as Phil Hill escapes the attentions of the crowd. He recovered to receive the winners' spoils alongside the dapper Belgian, Gendebien, who has clearly had time to wash and change into his glad rags. It was a good year for Hill: he went on to win the Formula 1 World Championship, also for Ferrari.

This is what Le Mans is all about: the start. Graham Hill, second from left, was first away on this occasion at the wheel of the Aston Martin DP212.

This is one of my favourite Le Mans shots. The year is 1962 and Olivier Gendebien is well on his way to scoring his second successive victory with Phil Hill and the Ferrari team – running the new 4-litre 330LM on this occasion. This picture was taken on Sunday morning, when the excitement of the first few hours and the drama of the night has given way to a certain weariness as the race enters its final phase.

The winning car is driven back to the pits after the finish with the triumphant Ferrari mechanics milking the applause. It was Maranello's sixth Le Mans victory, surpassing the record shared by Bentley and Jaguar.

More smiles from the winners' rostrum in 1963 as Scarfiotti and Bandini – the first all-Italian crew to win Le Mans – celebrate Ferrari's seventh 24-hour victory. They were joined on the podium by Graham Hill and Richie Ginther, who had debuted the innovative Rover-BRM gas turbine car. Running outside the regulations, but with the blessing of the organisers, the Rover-BRM completed the full race distance and finished in an unofficial seventh place. Ten years earlier the Automobile Club de l'Ouest had offered a 25,000 franc prize for the first turbine-engined car to complete the distance. The boys from Solihull had risen to the challenge in fine style.

Le Mans by night takes on an atmosphere all of its own, and the pits in particular is a good place for evocative photographs. This is 1964, and the Lindner–Nocker E-type Jaguar is in for a new cylinder head gasket.

The very Gallic-looking man on the right was the Chief Marshal at *Whitehouse*, which was one of my favourite places for Le Mans pictures. I would usually head out there on Sunday morning, and was often bemused by the sight of the paperboy sprinting across the track carrying a huge bag of newspapers destined for those houses on the inside of the circuit.

On this occasion the marshal led me to a point further up the track – where the cars were travelling at their fastest – because he reckoned it was a good place for pictures. He assured me it was perfectly safe although you will notice that he stood quite far back. This shot of Graham Hill in Colonel Ronnie Hoare's Maranello Concessionaires-entered Ferrari 330P was one of the results.

By the middle of the 1960s Le Mans was all about the battle between Ferrari and Ford. Here they are during the 1965 race eyeball-to-eyeball on the *Mulsanne* travelling at speeds in excess of 190mph. In fact the more I think about it, the more impressed I am with myself for getting both these cars in the same frame! On the nearside is the all-American effort of a Shelby-prepared GT40 driven by AJ Foyt and Phil Hill. The Ferrari is in the capable hands of David Piper and Jo Bonnier. Both were factory-entered teams but in the end it was the NART (North American Racing Team) Ferrari of Jochen Rindt and Masten Gregory which won the day.

Arnage corner on Sunday: a chance to read the morning papers and perhaps find out who is leading the race going on just behind you.

It rained at Le Mans too of course, and when it did it was a rotten place to be traipsing around with your camera bag. The pits was generally the best place to be under such circumstances and the driver changes – such as this one between Pedro Rodriguez and Ritchie Ginther – usually provided a good opportunity for photographs.

More action from the Ferrari pit – this is 1967 – as Scarfiotti, standing on the left, hands over to Mike Parkes and the mechanic sends the P4 on its way to an eventual second place overall behind the Gurney/Foyt GT40. It's incredible to see so many people – hangers-on most of them – milling around with their hands in their pockets, and you'll notice that the barrier between the pits and the main straight is yet to be built.

Exactly one week after Le Mans came the Reims 12 Hours. It was a relatively minor event in the grand scheme of things but it was definitely one of the most enjoyable to cover from my point of view because the pressure-cooker atmosphere of Le Mans was over and everyone was more relaxed. The race started at 11pm and the evenings were usually warm and dry. With the tripod set up in the grand-stand and the shutter speed set for a quarter of a second I could often get a decent picture of the start despite the darkness. This sequence was shot in 1967.

All is calm before the flag drops, and then chaos descends upon the circuit as the cars explode into life and scream into the distance with their headlights blazing.

It was, of course, entirely appropriate that the winners should celebrate with the local beverage and on this occasion – 1965 – it was the Mexican star Pedro Rodriguez, on the left, and Jean Guichet who emerged victorious.

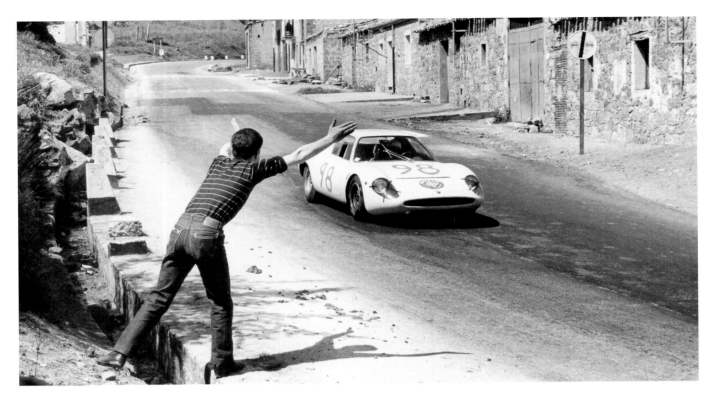

It was every motoring photographer's ambition to cover the Targa Florio at least once during their career. I was lucky enough to be sent on two occasions – in 1967 and 1973. The latter year was the last time it was run as a World Championship event. The exact route varied considerably over the years but by 1967 it had settled on the classic format of ten laps of a 71.4km circuit based around the start-finish straight near the village of Cerda. Like the Mille Miglia, it embodied everything the Italians love about motor sport. This picture of a boy waving while a potent little Abarth (driven by Guido Garufi and Giuseppe Ferlito) races past pretty much sums up what it was all about: poorly-maintained public roads, state-of-the-art racing cars and wildly-enthusiastic spectators.

I got this shot of the Taramazzo-Bona Porsche 906 after being invited up into someone's flat where the customary Targa party was in full swing. The flat was full of people; the pasta was bubbling away and I managed to squeeze through to the balcony to get a bird's-eye view of the 'track'. Note the small radio in the foreground: this was the only way people could keep in touch with the progress of the race.

This is as about an incongruous picture as I will ever take. The sophisticated Chaparral-Chevrolet 2F set against the rocky backdrop of the Sicilian mountains. Phil Hill and 'Hap' Sharp hustled the winged monster as high as fourth place overall before a puncture on lap nine ruined any chances of overall success.

The Ford France-entered GT40 (Henri Greder and Jean Michel Giorgi) thunders between the classical walls and towers of Campofelice. The roads were closed first thing in the morning and so, the night before the race, I slept in the car somewhere up on the circuit.

Another hard day watching the Targa Florio, although how these two managed to sleep through the noise of that GT40 racing past I shall never know.

The most attractive town on the circuit was probably Collesano, which was the last village before the fast descent back down to the coast. Threading his way across the bridge and out of the town is the pipe-smoking Italian, Umberto Maglioli, who won the Targa outright on two previous occasions – for Lancia in 1953 and for Porsche in 1956. He would complete the hat-trick in 1968, sharing a works Porsche 907 with Vic Elford.

I've always loved this shot. The balconies and doorways are packed with cheering humanity as the Scuderia Filipinetti Ferrari P4 driven by Jean Guichet and Herbert Muller tears down what is usually a quiet high street. The Sicilians loved all the cars on the Targa, but nothing got them going quite as much as a red Ferrari ripping up their tarmac.

The most exciting finish in the history of Le Mans came in 1969, when Jackie Oliver and Jacky Ickx's Gulf-JW Ford GT40 finished just 12 yards ahead of the Hermann–Larousse Porsche 908. The great irony of this race was that Ickx, in protest against the continued use of the running start at Le Mans, had strolled across to his car and carefully belted himself in. How close would the finish have been had he not given away so much time at the start?

We made it! A jubilant Oliver and Ickx on the podium.

Heat haze signals the start of the 1972 International Trophy at Silverstone. Jackie Stewart's distinctive Elf-sponsored Tyrrell is at the head of the pack. John Surtees and Chris Amon are on his right, with Ronnie Peterson's March looking for a gap from the third row.

FORMULA 1

Ken Tyrrell and Jackie Stewart seem to be searching for the winner's rostrum at the end of the 1970 Brands Hatch Race of Champions. Their grip on the victory circle between 1969 and 1973 was vice-like, producing three world titles for the Scot and a Constructors' Championship for Tyrrell.

A thoughtful Jacky Ickx: superb driver and a thoroughly decent bloke. My colleague Geoff Goddard tells a revealing tale about the Belgian. Geoff was struggling back to the UK from Spa on the notorious motorway between Liège and Brussels. It was considered one of the most dangerous stretches of road in Europe, with persistent road works and contra-flow systems. On this occasion it was pouring with rain and the conditions were lethal. Geoff was second-guessing his way through the spray in a Cortina when Ickx pulled alongside in his 911. He waved to Geoff to follow him and then took the lead. He guided Geoff through the murk, weaving in and out of the traffic, at just the right speed for Geoff to keep on his tail. This impromptu convoy reached Brussels (and a safer road) without incident; Ickx waved 'goodbye' and disappeared off up the road.

After one year out Matra returned to the Formula 1 fray with the new V12-engined MS120 driven by Jean-Pierre Beltoise and Henri Pescarolo. 'Pesca' was more of a sports car man, I suppose, winning Le Mans three times between 1972 and 1974.

The start of the Monaco Grand Prix is always a good place for an exciting picture. I would normally go somewhere like *Mirabeau* or the harbour but on this occasion I stayed at *St Devote*. It's incredible how many people there are just hovering by the barriers completely unprotected, as if they are waiting for a bus. This was the famous race in 1970 when Jochen Rindt got past Jack Brabham's failing BT33 on the last corner of the last lap to win the race. As usual I was halfway to England with my films by then.

Two fearless fighters in their element. This is the 'Mexican Bandit' – Pedro Rodriguez – and the 'Crazy Swiss' – Jo Siffert – hurtling down to *Mirabeau*. I particularly like this shot because they are not fighting for the lead or even a place in the top three. In fact, they finished the race in just sixth and eighth place respectively, but you can be sure they would have fought every inch of the way.

Even the master of Monaco gets it wrong from time to time. Five times winner Graham Hill steps from the wreck of his Lotus 49C during practice for the 1970 race. This was his first return to the Principality since the horrific accident at Watkins Glen in 1969 where he broke both legs. Amazing as it may seem today he was actually driving the same car at Monaco with which he won the previous year's race. It had been bought from Lotus and entered by Rob Walker. Hill recovered from this practice mishap to finish fifth on race day.

Belgian Grand Prix weekend, 1970. From the left, Jackie Stewart, Jochen Rindt, Rob Walker, John Miles (Rindt's team-mate) and Graham Hill share a joke. About what I cannot say…

The driving force of the 1970 Grand Prix season was, once again, Team Lotus. Jochen Rindt and Colin Chapman seem to be eyeing up the opposition prior to Rindt's victory at Zandvoort in the sensational new Lotus 72. It was a race tainted by tragedy, however, when Rindt's close friend, Piers Courage, was killed at the wheel of his de Tomaso-Cosworth. It is often said that Courage's death, following so closely after Bruce McLaren's fatal accident at Goodwood, had a serious psychological impact on Rindt. There was even talk of retirement, despite the fact that he was well on course to take the World Championship. I suppose we will never know for sure. Rindt himself was killed during practice for that year's Italian Grand Prix, winning the title posthumously.

The drivers' partners tended to stick together, more often than not to share worries and – at worst – to grieve. The dangers of the sport were a powerful bond. Among the wives and girlfriends here are Nora Tyrrell, wife of Ken, on the left and Bette Hill, wife of Graham, on the right. It was Bette, together with Betty Brabham and Pat McLaren, who formed 'the Doghouse Club' – a support group for bereaved widows and girlfriends.

Posing on the pit wall: Stewart, Oliver and Hill at Clermont Ferrand in 1970.

A young Frank Williams confers with Brian Redman during practice for the 1970 British Grand Prix. Frank was a slick operator in the early days, but then you needed to be in order to survive. On this occasion the Cosworth-powered de Tomaso 505 did not even start the race because a broken half-shaft could not be replaced in time. It is hard to imagine that happening at Williams today!

Another new star joins the Grand Prix firmament. All the ladies loved the handsome Frenchman, François Cevert, and he could drive well too. Here he is in Ken Tyrrell's March 701 in 1970, exploring the lines available at *Druids* hairpin. He was a loyal lieutenant to Jackie Stewart and a willing protégée of the triple Champion. His career was tragically cut short when he was killed at Watkins Glen in 1973.

Smoother lines from race leaders Jochen Rindt and Jack Brabham during the same event. Rindt had luck on his side that day: Brabham had passed him in the BT33 and seemed set for victory when he ran out of fuel on the last lap, leaving Rindt to collect the win.

World Champion-elect Rindt and reigning Champion Jackie Stewart. I took this before the start of the German Grand Prix, which Rindt went on to win. The headline in the following week's *The Motor* read 'Jochen's Year?' This seems a tragically accurate prediction in retrospect.

German fans adapt to their surroundings at Hockenheim.

Jacky Ickx (Ferrari 312B) leads at the end of the first lap of the German Grand Prix. This is always an exciting moment at Hockenheim. The field disappears off into the forest for most of the lap and it is only when they enter the stadium complex at the end of it that you know who is leading – at least that was the case before the giant TV screens came along. For this shot I had positioned myself at the end of the 180mph straight just before the complex. I had felt pretty safe behind what I thought was a concrete barrier, until I leant on it and realised that it was made of polystyrene.

A common sight at Monza in the 1960s and early 1970s was a train of Grand Prix cars hurtling down the main straight dancing in and out of one another's slipstream. That's Pedro Rodriguez leading in the Yardley-BRM P153, with Chris Amon's March 701-Cosworth on the left and Jackie Stewart, also in a March, just behind. Shadowing them all in the fourth-placed Ferrari is the eventual winner, Clay Regazzoni. This was 'Regga's' maiden win – a good place to do it when you drive for Maranello – and it went a small way to lifting everyone's spirits after Rindt's fatal practice crash.

The infamous tunnel under Loews Hotel at Monaco. I wouldn't normally get to this point of the track during the race – it was too far from the main road to the airport – but this is practice for the 1971 race and the Tyrrell 001 of Jackie Stewart is stamping his authority on the Grand Prix grid once again. He took pole in the rain and won the race from the front. It was a typically dominant performance in a year when he and the Tyrrell team won both drivers and constructors championships.

Looking not unlike a Roman emperor, the Italian-born American Mario Andretti makes one of his guest appearances for Ferrari at the 1971 Monaco Grand Prix. Torn between racing commitments on both sides of the Atlantic, Andretti had won his first Grand Prix at Kyalami at the beginning of that season but it wasn't until 1975 that he made the switch to Formula 1 on a full-time basis.

Graham Hill's last Formula 1 victory was the Daily Express Trophy at Silverstone in 1971, driving the Brabham BT34. His Grand Prix career as a driver was in gentle decline by this point although the Embassy project lay ahead.

Graham and Bette Hill assume their customary roles: Graham about to start another race and Bette on the time sheets. A foot operation had left her in plaster for six weeks, but she still went to the races.

The French circuit of Paul Ricard was a bleak and barren venue compared to the picturesque Clermont Ferrand, and when the Grand Prix circus visited this new 'racing facility' for the first time in 1971 the photographers among us were disappointed with the possibilities for taking decent pictures. This shot of Denny Hulme's McLaren M19A is a fairly typical Ricard view.

Probably the only good thing about Paul Ricard was Bandol, the pretty bucket and spade town where everyone stayed. The Tyrrell team used to hire a boat for entertaining sponsors and guests and I was walking past one day when I spotted Ken contemplating the water. On further enquiry it turned out that he had dropped his glasses over the side.

The 1971 Italian Grand Prix was the last great slipstream battle before the introduction of chicanes at Monza slowed everyone down. At an average speed of 150.75mph it also still stands as the fastest Grand Prix ever. Here the luckless Kiwi, Chris Amon, leads in his Matra-Simca, followed by François Cevert (Tyrrell), Mike Hailwood (Surtees) and Ronnie Peterson (March). This high-speed train, which also included men like Siffert, Stewart, Regazzoni, Ickx and the BRM pairing of Peter Gethin and Howden Ganley, continued to swap positions throughout the race. Amon, who looked odds-on to finally break his Grand Prix duck, was denied victory yet again when his visor flew off and he finished a disappointed sixth. It was in fact Gethin who took a surprising victory, slipstreaming to greatest effect at the last corner to outfumble Peterson, Cevert, Hailwood and Ganley. The first five were covered by just 0.61sec.

The young Brazilian, Emerson Fittipaldi *(right)*, unexpectedly found himself the team leader at Lotus after Rindt's death. He handled the pressure with great maturity, taking his first Grand Prix victory in only his fourth race and winning the World Championship in 1972 and 1974.

Torrential rain at Monaco in 1972 saw the form book turned on its head when Jean-Pierre Beltoise won for BRM, beating the acknowledged wet weather ace, Jacky Ickx, as well as Fittipaldi, who is pictured here in the Lotus 72D climbing the hill to *Casino Square*. This race was probably the closest I have ever got to missing my deadline. Fellow photographer Geoff Goddard and I had decided to book a taxi to take us to the airport rather than take a hire car as we usually did. Unfortunately the race ran late because of the rain and we missed the taxi. We eventually hitched a ride to the airport in a battered old 2CV that was used to carry vegetables to the Loews Hotel kitchens.

This picture of the start of the 1972 Spanish Grand Prix at Jarama was taken from the top of the main grandstand, which gave you a good view of this very dull circuit. That's Denny Hulme streaking away in the McLaren from second on the grid. Stewart and Fittipaldi slip past Ickx's slow-starting Ferrari.

François Cevert leads Hulme at Montjuich Park in 1973. Cevert's team leader Jackie Stewart – in his last season before retirement – was the first to admit that Cevert was quicker than him in some of the mid-season races. Cevert was being groomed to assume the Tyrrell leadership after Stewart's retirement, but his fatal crash at Watkins Glen left the team in turmoil.

This is how I like to remember Montjuich Park: beautiful old buildings, derelict mansions and hundreds of people perched on the banks lining the track – and of course a string of Grand Prix cars picking their way between it all. Fittipaldi's win here in the 72E was the 50th for the Lotus marque.

Ronnie Peterson carried the torch for drivers cast in the heroic mould through most of the 1970s. He was a spectacular driver and a nice bloke who simply loved racing and knew no speed other than flat-out. He came close to winning the World Championship on a couple of occasions but more often than not he seemed to be let down by his machinery. Not that it seemed to bother him: he just loved to drive cars fast. I was there at the start of the Italian Grand Prix in 1978 and did take some pictures of the aftermath of his accident, but I would never want to see them published. His death in hospital the following morning was such a shock; everyone thought that he was going to pull through.

When you see someone on three wheels at Monaco of all places then you know that they must really be going for it. This is 1973 and Jackie Stewart is about to notch up his 25th Grand Prix victory, surpassing the total won by his countryman, Jim Clark, and firmly placing Scotland at the very pinnacle of motor racing.

This view of the new *Rascasse* hairpin was taken from the roof of the medical unit. I was quite pleased with this picture because it reminds you that there is more to Monaco than just a tunnel of barriers.

For the 1973 Belgian Grand Prix, the Formula 1 circus moved to Zolder, dispensing with Spa-Francorchamps as a result of an internal wrangle between the two circuits' French and Flemish-speaking owners. Unfortunately, the track started breaking up almost as soon as everyone arrived and Jackie Stewart made a point of taking us all round to see. Jackie's safety campaign was in full swing by now and the reactionaries began complaining that he would produce 'Mickey Mouse circuits for Mickey Mouse drivers'. It was during our tour of the Zolder track that my friend Geoff Goddard pulled out his Mickey Mouse-shaped camera and took a picture of Jackie who, I am relieved to say, took the joke very well. There is no doubt that many of the great circuits were emasculated by the new safety regulations but by the same token there are certainly many more older drivers now enjoying retirement than there would have been.

Keeping an eye on their loved ones are Helen Stewart, right, and, below, Bette Hill (sitting with Jack Oliver and his wife Lynn) at Paul Ricard in 1973.

It took me ages to set this shot up. I was trying to organise a group photograph for Goodyear but the drivers were either chatting among themselves or they would keep sloping off. Yours truly was stuck on the roof screaming at everyone to stand still and smile. It was a good weekend, though, because Ronnie Peterson finally scored his first win.

United we stand. There was controversy in Austria in 1973, when the Grand Prix Drivers Association attempted to restrict pit lane access to drivers, mechanics and team principals only. This obviously put the press association's nose out of joint and led to the entire press corps blocking the pit lane at the start of practice. Clay Regazzoni, who was less sensitive to these matters than some of the drivers, simply put his foot down and sent all the journos running for cover. Mike Hailwood, however, stalled while trying to thread his way slowly past – and here we all are locked in a stalemate!

GALLERY 1967–78

Zandvoort, 1967: BRM Chief Mechanic Cyril Atkins.

Zandvoort, 1967: Team Lotus boss Colin Chapman, with drivers Jim Clark and Graham Hill.

Monza, 1967: Bruce McLaren casts an eye over the Eagle-Weslake.

Targa Florio, 1967: Enzo Buzzetti and Secondo Ridolfi,
Abarth 1000.

Targa Florio, 1967: Dan Margulies and Robert Mackie,
Porsche 911S.

Zandvoort, 1969: Jochen Rindt – in temporary helmet – in the Lotus 49B.

British Grand Prix winners in 1969: Jackie Stewart and the Matra MS80.

Silverstone, 1969: Chris Amon hoods up (Ferrari 312).

A man with a lot on his mind. Bruce McLaren, in a McLaren, before the 1969 Race of Champions.

The majesty of Clermont Ferrand: 1970 French Grand Prix.

Clermont Ferrand, 1970. World Champion Jackie Stewart (Tyrrell-entered March 701) leads Jo Siffert ('factory' March) onto the grid.

Clermont Ferrand, 1970. Dan Gurney
(carrying helmet), McLaren M14A

Jacky Ickx, Ferrari 312B, in the pits at
Clermont, 1970.

Montjuich Park, 1971: Emerson Fittipaldi, Lotus 72.

Reigning Champion Jackie Stewart, Tyrrell 003, wins the 1972 French Grand Prix.

The charms of Campofelice welcome the Targa Florio, 1973.

Zolder, 1976: James Hunt (McLaren M23) in his World Championship year.

Zolder, 1976: Clay 'Regga' Regazzoni, Ferrari 312T2.

Brands Hatch, 1976: Jody Scheckter in the Tyrrell P34 six-wheeler.

Jarama, 1976: Emerson Fittipaldi, in the Fittipaldi FD04.

Le Mans, 1976. The winning Porsche 936 of Jacky Ickx and Gijs van Lennep.

Monza, 1977: Patrick Depailler (Tyrrell P34) leads Jacques Laffite (Ligier JS7)

Champion again. Niki Lauda at Monza, 1977.

Le Mans, 1978: Renault's year.

Jackie Stewart survived a career in Formula 1 between 1965 and 1973, arguably its most dangerous period. He came in for a lot of stick for insisting that the sport be made safer but more than any driver alive today he knew precisely what he was talking about.

New kid on the block – or, rather, the harbour. Clay Regazzoni leads his new teammate, the Austrian Niki Lauda, at Monaco in 1974. When he joined Ferrari at the beginning of the year Lauda quickly asserted himself as the leading driver, winning in Spain and Holland and capturing the World Championship twice during the next four years.

On two occasions during the first half of the 1970s the Belgian Grand Prix was held at the singularly uninspiring circuit of Nivelles, close to the Waterloo battlefield. It was flat and featureless and there was never anywhere good for pictures. This is the pre-race drivers' briefing in 1974 and Brian Redman, standing behind Graham Hill, has just played his old trick of removing his false front teeth, baring his gums at us and then closing his mouth before we could take a picture! The most memorable thing about the race was the fact that the organisers played the Abba song *Waterloo* non-stop for almost the entire weekend. It drove us all crazy.

Graham Hill poses with his Embassy-Hill cars at Zolder in 1975. The team struggled to make the grade in Formula 1, although the arrival of new young star Tony Brise at the beginning of the season offered a glimmer of hope for the future. All that was lost on the approach to Elstree Airfield the following November, when Hill, Brise and four members of the team were killed when their plane crashed in thick fog.

The 1975 Spanish Grand Prix at Montjuich Park began, and ended, under a cloud and we were never to return there again. When the teams arrived at the circuit there was general horror at the state of the Armco barriers, many of which were not even bolted down properly. When the drivers refused to race the organisers threatened to lock the entire paddock in the football stadium where they were based. Order of some sorts was resumed when it was agreed that the barriers would be repaired in time for practice to start. For some publicity-conscious team managers, such as Colin Chapman (right), the opportunity was too good to miss and he mucked in to help. The striking drivers pictured above are, from left, Rolf Stommelen on the bike, Niki Lauda, Jody Scheckter, Emerson Fittipaldi and James Hunt. The race did go ahead, but it ended in tragedy when the rear wing strut on Stommelen's Embassy-Hill failed and sent him spinning into the crowd, killing four spectators. It was another example of the new generation of cars outpacing the limitations of a supremely picturesque venue.

Niki Lauda won five Grands Prix (including this one at Paul Ricard) and nine pole positions in 1975 to claim the first of his three World Championships. Had it not been for his accident at the Nürburgring in 1976, he might have won a hat-trick of titles for Ferrari.

One of the more memorable moments in the history of the British Grand Prix at Brands Hatch taken, I might add, without the benefit of a motor wind on my trusty Leica. Lauda and team mate Clay Regazzoni tangle at Paddock while Lauda's principal rival for the title, James Hunt, is launched over the second Ferrari's rear wheel. Lauda survived the incident but Hunt's steering was terminally damaged. The race was stopped. Hunt parked his stricken car behind the pits on *Cooper Straight* and then went and jumped into the spare and waited for the restart. That's when things started getting complicated. The stewards argued that, in order to be eligible for the re-start, drivers had to have completed the first lap – which Hunt clearly hadn't. When it seemed likely that Hunt wouldn't be allowed to start his home race the crowd went absolutely beserk; people started cat-calling and throwing beer cans onto the track. The organisers had to let him start; there would have been a riot otherwise. He went on the win the race – beating Lauda – and the 1976 World Championship, although his points won at Brands were taken away later in the year.

The 1976 Italian Grand Prix marked Niki Lauda's return to Formula 1 just eight weeks after his horrific accident at the Nürburgring. His drive to fourth place – which included the second fastest lap of the race – made him an instant hero in the eyes of the adoring *tifosi*.

South African star Jody Scheckter heads John Watson's Alfa-powered Brabham BT45, which had started from pole, on his way to victory at Monaco in 1977 in the brand new Wolf WR1. It would also be the 100th Grand Prix win for the Ford-Cosworth V8, although to me it didn't seem that long ago that Jimmy Clark was winning the 1967 Dutch Grand Prix to notch up the company's first.

More action from the same race. The first four: Scheckter, Watson, Carlos Reutemann and Hans Stuck have all gone through. Hot on their heels is Ronnie Peterson's Tyrrell P34, Niki Lauda's Ferrari 312T2, James Hunt's McLaren M23, Patrick Depailler in the second Tyrrell and Mario Andretti's Lotus 78.

From time to time in Formula 1 the relationship between a driver and his team boss can produce the most outstanding results. Colin Chapman and Jim Clark had that kind of bond and so did Niki Lauda and Ferrari boss Luca di Montezemolo, pictured here during Lauda's first Championship year.

The *tifosi* at Monza. Just watching the fans arrive on race morning was an experience to be cherished. Their determined approach was as for an army assault course. They would be carrying ropes, trenching tools and bolt cutters and often gave the impression of having spent several weeks in training. They would dig under the fence, cut through it or climb over it – any which way save through the gate itself. I once watched one man climb the sheer face of the main grandstand to make it onto the roof, a feat that earned him a roaring ovation from the watching crowd. Even the police were so impressed that they let him stay there. On one memorable weekend an articulated lorry arrived in the public car park, swung down its doors and – for a few *lira* – offered its storage space as a shelter from the rain for scooters and mopeds. Plenty of people took up the offer and the lorry was quickly full to capacity. Once the race was underway the lorry pulled up its doors and was gone!

Mario Andretti and Colin Chapman enjoyed a close rapport which was cemented throughout 1978 when the revolutionary 'ground-effect' Lotus 79 proved virtually unbeatable.

Niki Lauda gives his new Brabham a disapproving look before the 1979 season-opener in South Africa, one of the last races I covered. The, by then, double World Champion would retire – for the first time – halfway through the season although he would return to enjoy more success with McLaren.

Blast off. Two of the definitive sports cars of the 1970s – the Group 5 Porsche 935 and the Group 6 'prototype' Porsche 936 – are silhouetted by the glare from their own headlights as they embark upon yet another lap of the Le Mans circuit.

THE SEVENTIES

SPORTS CARS

A rain-soaked Brands Hatch plays host to Britain's round of the World Sports Car Championship, the BOAC 1000 kms. The year is 1970. The JW Automotive-Gulf Porsche 917 piloted by Jo Siffert and Brian Redman picks its way gingerly past the back-markers. The race was something of a Porsche benefit. Pedro Rodriguez and Leo Kinnunen won the day, while the more-fancied Ferraris were beaten by rain and electrical problems.

These big cars look somehow incongruous on Brands' narrow track, particularly as they negotiate *Druids*. The 917 diving down the inside of Muller's Ferrari 512 was driven by Vic Elford and Denny Hulme. The conditions were so bad that it seemed possible that the race would run beyond the Kent track's 7pm curfew. Fortunately, the winning car completed the distance with 15 minutes to spare.

In your face motor sport: the Porsche 908 of Hans Dieter Dechent, Gerhard Koch and Gerard Larousse dives into *Paddock*.

After Stirling Moss, perhaps, you could argue that Derek Bell was Britain's most talented sports car driver. Certainly, his five wins at Le Mans give him the most impressive record there of any driver bar his friend and former team-mate, Jacky Ickx. I was surprised that he never made it in Formula 1. His brief spell with Scuderia Ferrari, 1968-69, came to nothing – through no real fault of his own. Drives with Surtees and Tecno also failed to reap the necessary dividends and Derek concentrated instead on sports cars. Formula 1's loss was definitely the World Sports Car Championship's gain.

The awesome Porsche 917 dominated sports car racing in the early 1970s, winning at Le Mans in 1970 and 1971. The winning Martini car pictured here was driven by an Austro-Dutch partnership, Helmut Marko and Gijs van Lennep, which held the Attwood/Muller Gulf-entered car at bay for the last nine hours. Two of Porsche's leading 917 performers, Jo Siffert and Pedro Rodriguez, were killed within a few weeks of one another – Rodriguez at the Norisring and Siffert at Brand Hatch – and, to some degree, the factory's ambitions for the car died with them.

Plastic table cloths, cups, ashtrays and bottles of Evian water: it could only be Le Mans and, in this case, the drivers' rest tent in 1972. Former Ferrari Formula 1 drivers Mike Parkes and Chris Amon chat over a stale baguette and strong coffee. Parkes enjoyed his greatest successes – including victories at Sebring, Spa and Le Mans – in sports cars. Tragically, he was killed in a road accident in Italy in 1977.

The fleet Matra-Simcas came as a breath of fresh air after the domination of Porsche, Ford and Ferrari. The French outfit won at Le Mans three times in succession, on each occasion with the crowd's favourite, Henri Pescarolo, partnering first Graham Hill, in 1972, and then Gérard Larrousse, in 1973–1974. This shot is of the Jabouille/Migault car, which finished third in 1974. The noise those Matra V12s made was earth-shattering, and I seem to recall that it was at about this time that I started using ear plugs when I went to races.

Running on empty? The 1975 race was blighted by the OPEC fuel crisis, forcing the Automobile Club de L'Ouest to restrict the size of the cars' fuel tanks and enforce a minimum of 20 laps between refuelling stops. The only engine capable of running both effectively and economically was the Cosworth DFV, making the race a straight fight between the two Gulf-Mirage GR8 DFVs driven by Derek Bell and Jacky Ickx (pictured leading at the start here) and Vern Schuppan and Jean-Pierre Jussaud. Bell and Ickx led almost from start to finish but with all those magnificent engines running in detuned form the whole event was something of an anti-climax.

Aussie driver Vern Schuppan lends a hand as Derek Bell straps himself into the JCB Mirage-Ford GR8 in preparation for another gruelling Le Mans stint. The year is 1976; fuel consumption restrictions had been abandoned and, for the first time, the Sports Car Championship was divided into Group 5 'silhouette' and Group 6 'prototype' classes with Porsche and Renault going head-to-head in both categories. Bell had tasted the winners' champagne for the first time the previous year, and would do so on four more occasions between 1981–1987. In 1976, however, he and Schuppan could manage only fifth overall.

Creeping past the old signalling pits just after *Mulsanne Corner*, competing cars head towards a blanket of smoke and dust that can only mean one thing. On this occasion, thankfully, there were no casualties apart from one flame-grilled Porsche. The Group 4-category Porsche turbos were generating in excess of 700 degrees at times, and on occasion they simply went up in flames. The smoke in this shot belongs to Hans Heyer's car; apparently the fire was tickling the back of his neck before he realised what was going on and made a swift exit.

The Hotel des Hunaudières, located about one third of the way down the three-mile *Mulsanne*, was a popular haunt for British fans. I became quite good friends with the owner over the years, and made regular visits to his bedroom in order to get a good view of the track – as shown in this picture. My trips upstairs became something of a standing joke between us, in true '*Allo? Allo?*' fashion. One of the best things about the restaurant was that you could sit at a table by the window and watch the cars race past while you ate. Conversation was a little tricky, due to the noise. The field opposite marks the spot where the Wright brothers made their first European flight.

Take your partners: Driver change for the Jarier/Schuppan Renault Mirage in 1977. Battle lines were drawn, once again that year, between Renault and Porsche. The Renault factory team – consisting of four Alpine A442s – was strong on paper but failed to last the distance. Their failure left French honour in the hands of the Mirages; Jarier and Schuppan finished second.

The ace up Porsche's sleeve in 1977 was Jacky Ickx. The Belgian, whose own Porsche 936 had retired early on, joined the sister Barth/Heywood car and drove an inspired race to catch and pass the two leading Mirage-Renaults, and notch up his third victory in succession (his fourth in total).

Jürgen Barth – whose father, Edgar, was a Porsche regular and previous winner of the Targa Florio – had the honour of driving the final few miles to victory. The car had broken a piston 45 minutes before the end of the race but, such was their lead over the rest of the field, they were able to remove a spark plug and complete two slow laps to win.

Approaching the halfway mark. The lonely life of the long distance *gendarme*.

Gallic pride was satisfied at last in 1978, when Didier Pironi and Jean-Pierre Jaussaud brought their Renault-Alpine A442B home five laps ahead of the nearest Porsche 936. The traditional Le Mans victory ceremony was even more chaotic than usual, and there was no way I was going to try and wade through *that* lot in order to get a close-up of the winners. This shot was taken from the relative safety of the main grandstand.

Mulsanne Corner, 1978: the third-placed Porsche 936 of Gregg/Heywood/Joest.

The clock shows 2pm. The dust, the heat haze and the string of *gendarmes* at trackside indicates that yet another Le Mans 24 Hours has got underway. The year is 1979 and my regular visits to the French classic are about to become rather less frequent. No regrets, though. I witnessed the best days of Jaguar, Ferrari, Ford, Matra and Porsche. I also saw the total distance covered in 24 hours rise from 4,088.06km (Rolt/Hamilton Jaguar C-type, 1953) to 5,332.79km (Lammers/Dumfries/Wallace Jaguar XJR-9LM, 1988).

I first visited Le Mans in 1953, joining *The Motor* photographer George Moore in his beloved Morris Oxford. Our journey to the circuit was delayed by a couple of days after George pitched the car off the road while testing the brakes (brake testing was something he believed all motorists should do on arrival in France). The radiator was destroyed in the accident and it was only with the help of the local *garagiste*, pictured here, that we were able to order a new one from Paris – delivered by train to the village where we were stranded. It was a nervous time for both of us since we only arrived at the track the night before the race and had missed practice completely. I couldn't help wondering at the time whether this was the sort of adventure that occurred *every* time you went abroad.

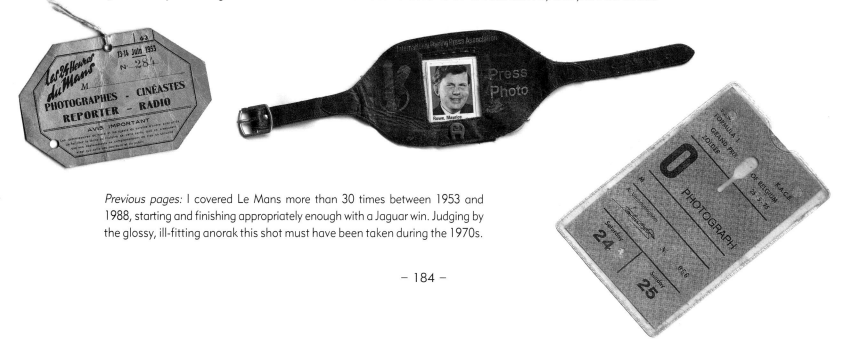

Previous pages: I covered Le Mans more than 30 times between 1953 and 1988, starting and finishing appropriately enough with a Jaguar win. Judging by the glossy, ill-fitting anorak this shot must have been taken during the 1970s.

Two views of the main straight at Reims, twenty-odd years apart. The shot above, taken in 1987 by Philip Turner, shows where I would stand in order to get the best view of the 11pm start, a view that has been somewhat obscured since. My favourite memory of Reims is of the Hotel Welcome. I recall Rodney Walkerley, *The Motor*'s Sports Editor, falling down the stairs of the hotel and breaking his leg. He was laid up in a hospital near the circuit and some of the drivers – Hawthorn and Collins among them – visited him after the race to give him a full report of what had happened so that Rodney could still file his story to the magazine.

Rally and sports car star Vic Elford made his Grand Prix debut at Rouen in 1969, driving a Cooper. Here he is that same weekend during an unscheduled trip across the grass and there am I on the extreme right of the picture taking the necessary avoiding action. All credit to Geoff Goddard for that shot. But it was also Elford who nearly ran me down on the Monte Carlo Rally, his Porsche 911 completing a slow rearwards slide towards the rockface against which I was pinned. I avoided injury by jumping on the car's bumper at the last minute. The bumper nudged the rocks, I jumped off, Elford selected first gear and drove away in complete ignorance of my presence. Missed again, Vic.

Perched on the shopping trolley outside Dr Muller's Sex Shop in Frankfurt Airport is that irrepressible rogue Innes Ireland, who was Grand Prix correspondent for *Autocar* and the first man to win a World Championship Grand Prix for Team Lotus. Innes was one of the old school of racing drivers, competing for the sheer love of the sport and with little or no thought of the direction his career might take. Apart from the racing, his remarkable life included periods as a paratrooper doing his National Service and, later, as the owner and captain of a fishing trawler in the North Sea. He is pictured here with, from left, photographers Nigel Snowdon, Peter Cramer and John Dunbar.

Freelance photographer Geoff Goddard *(centre)* was my travelling companion to and from many of the races for at least ten years. We were both active during roughly the same period, although he finally tired of living out of a suitcase during the mid-1970s. He has recently been made an honorary member of the British Racing Drivers Club.

The inimitable Denis 'Jenks' Jenkinson (foreground), freelance journalist and *Continental Correspondent* for the monthly *Motor Sport* magazine, pictured here with Henry Manney III, the American journalist. I count myself very lucky to have known 'Jenks' during his most active period as a journalist. He was a one-off, for sure, and his role in Stirling Moss' record-breaking 1955 Mille Miglia run – calmly reading pace notes from a roller while Moss drove at over 170mph – has entered into sporting legend.

Beryl and I were married in 1954. She single-handedly raised our three children while I was gallivanting around the Continent, something which she has every right never to let me forget. She did join me on the occasional job, such as this trip to Monza, but more often than not we simply ran up telephone bills.

My great friend and colleague, the late Philip Turner, who was Sports Editor at *The Motor*. He and I must have travelled the length and breadth of Europe several times over. This shot of him at Reims was taken in 1987, during one of our last visits to cover Le Mans.

Enzo Ferrari granted Philip and I an interview shortly after the Italian Grand Prix one year. Ferrari greeted Philip like an old friend, explaining that when he had heard that Mr Turner was in Modena he had cancelled all his morning appointments to make space for the interview. I remember rather tentatively asking Ferrari if it would be all right for me to take some pictures. To which he replied: 'For a friend of Mr Turner? Of course!' After a few minutes snapping away he held up his hands in submission and laughed: 'Enough! I am an old man and very tired!' That brief gesture resulted in one of my most memorable pictures.

During the winter months I would be dispatched to cover most of the major international rallies of the day. My first assignment was the 1960 Monte Carlo Rally, where I joined *The Motor*'s Editor Christopher Jennings, his wife Margaret (née Allen, who once held the Ladies Lap Record at Brooklands) and Philip Turner to travel four-up in this Vauxhall Cresta. The journey took three days and included stops at every *Michelin Guide*-recommended hotel and restaurant between Boulogne and Monte Carlo. In later years – when we weren't travelling with the boss – Philip and I would complete the journey in 12 hours. The most memorable moment of that first trip was arriving home late at night to discover my daughter Carol had been born.

Occasionally I would find myself in just the right place at just the right time. This is the Loch Ackray stage of the 1966 RAC Rally and the reigning Formula 1 World Champion Jim Clark has just planted his Lotus Cortina in the ditch. I had driven into the stage the night before and, armed with just a single blanket, settled down to what 'Jenks' would call a few 'zzzzs'. Come first light I was sorting out my cameras and anticipating the first cars through any minute when I heard this terrific crash. I hurried round the bend to find Jimmy – aided by a small but willing group of spectators – trying to manhandle the Cortina back onto the road. He retired from the event after that incident, but continued to turn up at service points and stage starts. He always had a smile on his face and the fans loved him for it.

Lunch on the Col de Turini for *(from left)* Mike Wood, Eric Carlsson, Tony Fall and *The Motor*'s young Rally Editor, Hamish Cardno. Hamish and I had been sent out to the Turini to watch the BMC team complete their winter testing and to do a feature on rising star Tony Fall. I had borrowed the BMC support car – a Renault 16 hire car – in order to follow Tony Fall's Mini and get some action shots. Unfortunately the Renault had bald tyres and I understeered into the side of the mountain. Everyone thought it was hilarious – except me – and I was only consoled when Carlsson arrived on the scene. Slapping me on the back he said: 'Maurice, with bald tyres and the Renault's umbrella handbrake there was no way anyone could have avoided that accident!'

Nairobi National Park, 1962. I was covering the East African Safari *(below)* with *Daily Herald* journalist Barrie Gill. A sudden and torrential storm left our Peugeot well and truly stranded in the middle of the African bush. I had to get some films on a plane to London that night, so I volunteered to set off on foot in search of help. I walked for at least three miles across the savannah, completely unprotected. The park rangers who rescued me thought I was mad – and they were probably right.

TEMPLE PRESS LTD

NEWSPAPER
PROPRIETORS
PRINTERS AND
PUBLISHERS

"THE MOTOR"
"THE LIGHT CAR"
THE
"COMMERCIAL MOTOR"
"THE AEROPLANE"
"MOTOR CYCLING"
"CYCLING"
"THE MOTOR BOAT"
"THE MOTOR SHIP"
"THE OIL ENGINE"
"PLASTICS"
"LIGHT METALS"

MANAGING DIRECTOR, ROLAND E. DANGERFIELD.
DIRECTOR AND GENERAL MANAGER, ROBERT ASHWORTH.

PLEASE REPLY TO:

BOWLING GREEN LANE
LONDON · E · C · I
TELEPHONE TERMINUS 3636
PRIVATE BRANCH EXCHANGE.
TELEGRAMS PRESSIMUS, SMITH, LONDON

HEAD   OFFICE:
LONDON
BOWLING GREEN LANE, E.C.I.

Also at

COVENTRY
50 · HERTFORD STREET

MANCHESTER
274 · DEANSGATE

TP/TDR/M

30th June, 1944

Mr. Maurice Rowe,
2 Childs Place,
Earls Court,
S.W.5.

Dear Mr. Rowe,

      Further to our conversation this morning, I can offer you a post as a junior in our Photographic Department at 32/6d per week, and, if satisfactory, 35/- at the end of one month's trial.

      I would point out that you will have every opportunity to learn Press Photography under the best conditions, and I shall be glad if you will call here again on Monday morning next as there may be an opening for you in another department if you do not accept the above offer.

Yours faithfully,

MANAGER
PHOTOGRAPHIC DEPARTMENT

And finally . . . This is the letter that started it all off.